COATS OF SKINS

A Treatise on the Salvation of Adam and Eve

By
David William Koster, D.D.

Author of
But for the Blood- A Treatise on the Blood of Christ
No More Sea- A Treatise on the Cessation of Evil
The Gospel in the Stars- A Treatise on the True Meaning of the Zodiac
The Last Trump – A Treatise on the Revelation of Jesus Christ to St. John

Copyright © 2018 David W. Koster. All rights reserved.

Writings contained herein are by the author unless otherwise stated.

No part of this publication may be reproduced, stored in a retrieval system or transmitted in any way by any means – electronic, mechanical, photocopy, recording or otherwise – without the prior permission of the copyright holder, except as provided by USA copyright law.

All Scriptures are taken from the King James Bible.

ISBN-13: 978-1722092580

Printed in the United States of America.

Acknowledgments

I would like to thank the faithful few who have yielded to the call to preach, forsook the riches of this world and have carried on the old time independent, fundamental, Authorized 1611 King James Bible preaching Baptist Ministry. Without these preachers of the true Word of God this soul would still be on its way to Hell.

I would also like to thank my wife for her strong belief in the Bible and for her support of my Bible studies.

DWK

Foreword

The Authorized 1611 King James Bible has been used exclusively for this treatise. The reason for this is, it is the only translation of the Holy Scriptures into the common man's language where **"The words of the LORD *are* pure words: *as* silver tried in a furnace of earth, purified seven times." (Psm 12:6).**

The proof that the 1611 King James Bible is the Word of God is that it possesses the qualities and powers that belong to such a Word. It is true; and being moral and spiritual truth, it appeals to one's sense of the truth, and approves itself to us. The truth that the 1611 King James Bible conveys is of the highest order and it kindles the mind that receives it to respond to its greatness.

King Henry VIII of England was the first and only sovereign Head of State to expunge the idolatrous and pagan influences of Roman Catholicism from his country. The British Parliament's passage of the 1534 A.D. Act of Supremacy deposed the Pope and established King Henry VIII and his successors as *"the only supreme head on earth of the Church of England"*. Then, as part of this purge of Popery, all their vast property holdings were confiscated and all their monasteries were shuttered.

The LORD showed His approval and support for the English Reformation and the concern the Royal Court had for the souls of its citizens by inspiring King James to have the Holy Scriptures translated into the common man's language. And to this day, the 1611 King James Bible remains the incontestable, true and inerrant word of God. The veracity of this translation has been validated by the LORD in several tangible and undeniable ways:

1. The LORD chose Greenwich, a district in Southeast London, as the site for the earth's Prime Meridian to highlight that the location where His Holy Word was translated into the common man's language is a prime terrestrial meridian: *a distinguished location that is first in rank, excellence, or significance, a unique location with no commonality to another.*

2. The LORD chose a Gentile nation as the site for the earth's Prime Meridian to highlight that the Gentile's meridian, *(brightest, highest, and crowning achievement),* is the 1611 King James Bible.

3. The establishment of a Prime Meridian for our planet at the location that coincides with the location where His Holy Word was translated into the common man's language signifies that the whole earth is measured in reference to God's Holy Scriptures.

4. The LORD's selection of the Royal Observatory as the site for the Prime Meridian serves as an ever-present reminder that **"they shall see the Son of man coming in a cloud with power and great glory" (Lk 21:28).**

5. The Prime Meridian is defined to be Zero degrees longitude, and because it coincides with the location where His Holy Word was translated into the common man's language it serves as a universal reminder that every person's walk in this life (mentally and physically) will be measured in relation to the Holy Scriptures.

6. Greenwich Meridian Time is the global time standard and because it coincides with the location where His Holy Word was translated into the common man's language it serves as a constant reminder that how we spent our time will

be judged in reference to God's Holy Word.

7. Every day begins and ends at the Prime Meridian which coincides with the location where His Holy Word was translated into the common man's language thereby reminding everyone that all our days on this earth are ordained by God.

Also, it is no coincident that upon adoption of the King James Bible the British Empire grew until the sun never set upon it. However, when the Church of England adopted the Revised Standard Edition Bible the British Empire started its downward slide and the Empire dissolved.

So, what more proof is needed that the 1611 King James Bible is the only book that **"*is* profitable for doctrine, for reproof, for correction, and for instruction in righteousness: That the man of God may be perfect, thoroughly furnished unto all good works." (2 Tim 3:16-17)**?

Coats of Skins

Introduction

The first book of the Bible entitled, *The First Book of Moses Called Genesis*, Chapter 3 and Verse 21 informs us that; **"Unto Adam also and to his wife did the LORD God make coats of skins, and clothed them."**

While this 18-word verse of Scripture can be read in less than 10 seconds, the author believes that it, as does every verse of Scripture, conveys tremendous truths. The author believes that it attests to the fact that Adam and Eve fully understood that they were under condemnation for transgression of God's Law. The author also believes that through the coat making process the LORD revealed His plan of salvation for mankind to Adam and Eve.

Additionally, it can be concluded that Adam and Eve passed their knowledge of God's plan of salvation on to their children. We know this to be true because both Cain and Able knew the requirement that a burnt offering needed to be made for their own sins for in "the process of time it came to pass, that Cain brought of the fruit of the ground an offering unto the LORD. And Abel, he also brought of the firstlings of his flock and of the fat thereof." (Gen 4:3-4).

By the making of the coats of skins, it is quite evident that from Adam and Eve on, man has known that "**the gospel of Christ is the power of God unto salvation to everyone that believeth**" **(Rom 1:16)**. It is also readily apparent that Jesus washes "**us from our sins in his own blood,**" **(Rev 1:5)** and the resultant regenerating effect salvation has on a mortal's soul was clearly conveyed.

And, because the LORD has instructed man on His plan of salvation, the LORD is well within His rights to expect that "**One generation shall praise thy [the LORD's] works to another, and shall declare thy mighty acts.**" **(Psm 145:4).** Therefore, all generations are without excuse and all should be able to proclaim:

"**Which we have heard and known, and our fathers have told us.**
We will not hide *them* from their children, shewing to the generation to come the praises of the LORD, and his strength, and his wonderful works that he

hath done.
*****

That the generation to come might know *them*, even the children *which* should be born; *who* should arise and declare *them* to their children: That they might set their hope in God, and not forget the works of God, but keep his commandments:" (Psm 78:3-4, 6-7).

It is acknowledged that the Scriptures do not explicitly state how the LORD God made coats of skins for Adam and Eve. Consequently, this treatise can be viewed as pure speculation. However, the author believes that the following proceedings can be surmised from Scripture and primitive leather processing methods. Hence, this treatise sets forth a probable way in which such coats of skins could have been made.

Admittedly, God could very well have spoken the coats of skins into existence however, the author believes this was not the case because, **"on the seventh day God ended his work which he had made; and he rested on the seventh day from all his work which he had made." (Gen 2:2).** Or, in other words, God had ceased from His creative actions.

For those who insist that the LORD God made the coats of skins personally, the author points out that the word *"make"* means *"to cause to be, to bring into being"*. Consequently, it is grammatically correct to interpret the verse to mean that the LORD God *"caused the coats to be* or *brought the coats into being"* via Adam.

In addition:
"Good and upright is the LORD: therefore will he teach sinners in the way." (Psm 25:8)
for **"Thus saith the LORD, thy Redeemer, the Holy One of Israel; I am *the* LORD thy God which teacheth thee to profit, which leadeth thee by the way *that* thou shouldest go." (Isa 48:17)**.

God also states that He is willing to instruct man in the ways of righteousness because He said:
"I will instruct thee and teach thee in the way which thou shalt go: I will guide thee with mine eye.
Be ye not as the horse, *or* as the mule, *which* have no understanding:" (Psm 32:8-9).
Consequently, it is believed that it was by this instruction that Adam learned that the LORD **"shall bring forth judgment unto truth." (Isa 42:2)**.

This is why in *The Gospel According to John*, Chapter 6, Verse 45 Jesus says:
"It is written in the prophets, And they shall be all taught of God. Every man therefore that hath heard, and hath learned of the Father, cometh unto me [Jesus]."

In the Beginning

In order to get the correct perspective on the need for the LORD to make Adam and Eve coats of skins, one must begin at man's beginning. The Bible informs us: **"In the beginning God created the heaven and the earth." (Gen 1:1).**

This is the first premise that every person must accept if they have any consideration for where their soul will spend eternity. Everyone who desires to spend eternity enjoying the splendors of Glory must come to a proper knowledge and correct understanding of exactly who God is and what He expects from every mortal.

There have been countless gods worshiped throughout the history of the world. However, the true and living LORD God presented to man via the

King James Bible "*is* greater than all gods: for in the thing wherein they dealt proudly *he was* above them." (Ex 18:11).

Many will reject this truth, but all should consider well what Paul the Apostle said, "*It is* **a fearful thing to fall into the hands of the living God.**" (Heb 10:31).

So remember:
"**The fear of the LORD is a fountain of life to depart from the snares of death.**" (Prov 14:27) and "**Whoso despiseth the word shall be destroyed:**" (Prov 13:13).

God's Commandment

The First Book of Moses Called Genesis, Chapter 1, Verse 27 informs us that on the sixth day of creation: "**God created man in his own image, in the image of God created he him; male and female created he them.**"

Hence, it is an incontestable fact that "**the LORD God formed man** *of* **the dust of the ground, and breathed into his nostrils the breath of life; and man became a living soul.**" (Gen 2:7).

Coats of Skins

The LORD placed man's eternal soul in a physical body to reside in while on this earth:
"Thou [the LORD] hast clothed me with skin and flesh, and hast fenced me with bones and sinews." (Job 10:11).

Hence Adam was a dualistic creation consisting of a spiritual body or commonly called a soul and a physical body which gives man the ability to interact in our three-dimensional world.

Each of these bodies, the flesh and the soul have a will or driving desires. The driving desire of the soul is fellowship with the Lord, its creator. The driving desires of the flesh are referred to in Scripture as "lusts". These three lusts are categorized as
1. The lust of the flesh: i.e. bodily wants
2. The lust of the eyes: i.e. bodily wants
3. The pride of life: i.e. bodily authority

How these lusts of the flesh manifest themselves depends upon a person's animating principle or *"spirit"*. In the Scriptures the word *"spirit"* is synonymous with *"soul"* however because each soul has a personality, it can, in many cases, denote a person's animating principle.

16

Each and every person, as well as many animals, have four animating principles. One animating principle predominates over the combination of the other three lesser animating principles. This is why Pit Bulls are highly aggressive and many race horses are *"high spirited"*. This fact also serves as one of the major lynch-pins underlying the bogus *"Science of Astrology"* and serves as a ready source of income to the multitude of *"Self-Help Gurus"*.

Today people refer to a person's animating principle as a Type A, B, C, or D personality while others refer to a person as being Dominant, Influential, Compliant or Steady.

The ancients believed that personality types paralleled the world's four fundamental elements:

Fundamental Element	Personality Type
Fire	Choleric
Air	Sanguine
Earth	Melancholic
Water	Phlegmatic

Coats of Skins

Choleric   Sanguine   Melancholic   Phlegmatic
Greek representation of the four animating principles of man

Hence when the Scriptures state that; **"The Spirit itself beareth witness with our spirit,"(Rom 8:16)** it is saying that the Holy Spirit bears witness not only to our soul but also to each and every personality type whether it be Choleric, Sanguine, Melancholic or Phlegmatic.

And, **"the grace of our Lord Jesus Christ be with your spirit."(Gal 6:18)** indicates that Jesus Christ's ever supportive and benevolent grace is extended to all regardless of whether they are primarily a Choleric, Sanguine, Melancholic or Phlegmatic person. This helps explain why the Lord can save anyone to the uttermost and why the Gospel has the power to comfort, uplift and invigorate every person on planet earth no matter what their situation or mental state is, bar-none.

A Treatise on the Salvation of Adam and Eve

It also needs to be noted that man was a creation unique from all other of God's creations. And while man was created a little lower than the Angels, man was created as a higher being than any animal due to the primary influence of the soul.

In fact, Adam was so unique that no other being could suffice as a perfectly compatible partner or an **"help meet for Adam"**. To rectify this situation God created a woman from one of Adam's ribs. Furthermore, we know that men and women are equal in God's eyes even though have been assigned different roles in this world, because the word Adam called Eve a *"woman"* or *"womb-man"*.

Now Adam and Eve, in their initial state were righteous and holy. We know this because *The First Book of Moses Called Genesis*, Chapter 3, Verse 8 informs us that God communed with Adam and Eve in the cool of the day. Unfortunately, Satan stirred up lusts of Eve's physical body and she was beguiled into believing that God was denying her an innate and inalienable right of knowing good and evil.
"For God doth know that in the day ye eat thereof, then your eyes shall be opened, and ye shall be as gods, knowing good and evil." (Gen 3:5).

Coats of Skins

Now the Lord places His Law for man's behavior (the Ten Commandments) in the heart of every man. We refer to this undeniable fact as our conscience. Sadly, the Devil's persuasive temptations made Eve discount the veracity of her conscience. And having no intellectual or experiential knowledge of death, Hell and the grave, she failed to appreciate the full ramifications of violating God's Law. Consequently, she **"took of the fruit thereof, and did eat, and gave also unto her husband with her; and he did eat." (Gen 3:6).**

The author speculates that Satan visited Eve on multiple occasions before she succumbed. More than likely she became enamored with Satan's magnetic personality and feigned magnificence seeing that he **"art the anointed cherub that covereth; and I have set thee so: thou wast upon the holy mountain of God; thou hast walked up and down in the midst of the stones of fire.**

Thou hast been in Eden the garden of God; every precious stone was thy covering, the sardius, topaz, and the diamond, the beryl, the onyx, and the jasper, the sapphire, the emerald, and the carbuncle, and gold: the workmanship of thy

tabrets and of thy pipes was prepared in thee in the day that thou wast created."(Ezek 28:14,13).

In other words, Satan was basically the equivalent of a modern day *"rock star"*. His raiment was sensational, his music was mesmerizing and his conviviality was captivating especially when he spoke of the ethereal grandeur that could be had when **"ye shall be as gods, knowing good and evil"(Gen 3"5).** And, just like young females today, Eve became *"star-struck"* with only shame and regret to show for her infatuation.

Eve ignored her conscience and yielded to the lusts of her flesh. The irreversible consequence was that her conscience was completely bowled over by the lusts of her flesh. Her flesh got dominion over her soul and to this day man's conscience is rarely listened to and for the most part totally ignored.

This fact that the natural man's flesh has dominion over his soul has recently been validated by Dr. Jonathan Corson. His research has found that our brains are actually wired for honesty, or in other words, the soul ever longs to be truthful and righteous.

Coats of Skins

His research has shown that when people feel they must needs lie, their mind first suppresses their conscience before uttering the falsehood.

Interestingly, this conflict between the soul and the flesh has adverse physiological effects as proven by a 2010 study by the Columbia University Graduate School of Business. This study demonstrated that dishonesty spikes cortisol levels, the body's primary stress hormone. In other words, the act of lying causes our bodies to pump out stress hormones as if we were in a *"fight or flight"* situation.

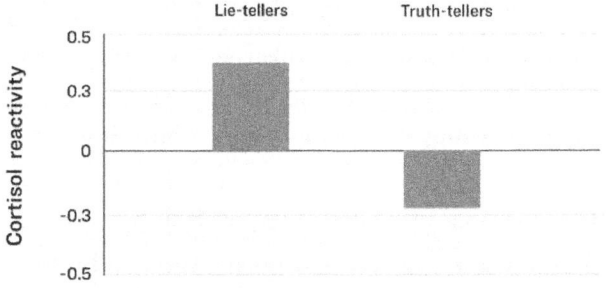

The result of the body's reaction to lying puts a strain on the cardiovascular system, increases inflammation, and may even lead to migraines. These physiological effects are why dishonesty is so emotionally and physically draining. And because lying is unholy **"all liars, shall have their part in the lake which burneth with fire and brimstone: which is the second death"(Rev 21:8).**

Dishonesty and Negative Health Outcomes

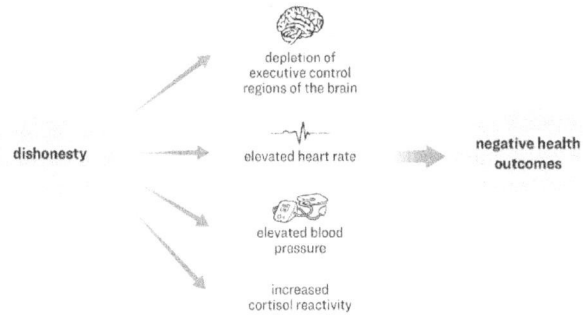

When Adam saw Eve's carnality it inflamed his physical lusts and his flesh rose to ascendency. He knew that he should **"cry unto the LORD in their trouble, and he [would] saveth them out of their distresses."(Psm 107:19)** but the lust of his flesh desired the same carnal passions Eve exhibited. The lust of his eyes desired his **"help meet"** in an intimate way and his pride of life made him think that he could be like a god and be the master of his own destiny. **"And Adam knew Eve his wife; and she conceived, and bare Cain,"(Gen 4:1).**

Coats of Skins

[The Scriptures do not indicate that Adam and Eve acted upon the LORD's command to **"be fruitful, and multiply, and replenish the earth,"(Gen 1:28)** until after their fall most likely due to the fact that their souls desire for fellowship with the LORD overrode the passions of their physical bodies.]

Sadly, Adam realized too late that carnality always begets more carnality. This is the reason why euphoria inducing drugs and viewing pornography are so addictive and create such an insatiable lust for more.

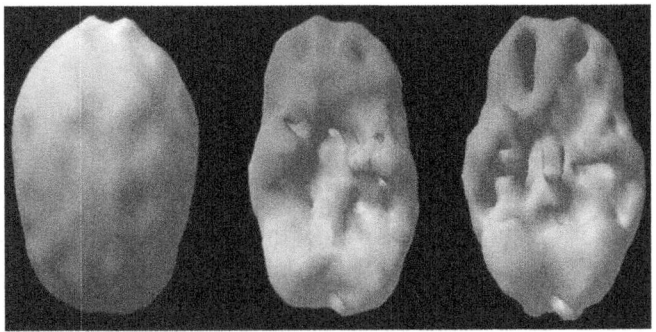

Normal Brain   Heroin's Affect   Porn's Affects

It is interesting to note that researchers have found that viewing pornography rots larger Swiss-cheese like holes in the brain's prefrontal cortex (the area for

24

high-order cognitive processes) than main-lining heroin. This fact has been documented via CAT-Scan images of the brain and explains the utter depravity exhibited by those who view such filth.

The end result was that Adam willingly partook of the forbidden fruit and disregarded the Lord's warning that **"in the day that thou eatest thereof thou shalt surely die." (Gen 2:16-17).**

As a result, of Adam's transgression of God's Law the flesh got the upper-hand over the soul because all mankind was in Adam when he violated God's Law and from that day **"the thoughts of man, that they are vanity"(Psm 94:11).**

Man's conscience would now be forever subservient to the lusts of the flesh. The consequence of their rebellion against God reduced mankind from being *"a little lower than angels"* to being *"a little higher than brute beasts"* and in many cases man is more savage than any beast. And lest anyone hold the mistaken notion that wealth and power elevates a person above the *"unwashed masses"* note what happened to Nebuchadnezzar the King of Babylon when God took away his higher-order cognition;
"he was driven from men, and did eat grass as

**oxen, and his body was wet with the dew of heaven, till his hairs were grown like eagles' feathers, and his nails like birds' claws.
And at the end of the days I Nebuchadnezzar lifted up mine eyes unto heaven, and mine understanding returned unto me, and I blessed the most High, and I praised and honoured him that liveth for ever, whose dominion is an everlasting dominion, and his kingdom is from generation to generation:"(Dan 4:33-34).**

The take away is that without Salvation, which with the help of the Holy Ghost reestablishes the soul's dominance over the lusts of the flesh, man is nothing more than a self-serving animal.

The realization that mankind was now lost and undone without God, drove Adam and Eve (and still drives mankind) to vainly attempt to cloak their unholiness. The Scriptures express this fact thusly: **"the eyes of them both were opened and they knew that they *were* naked; and they sewed fig leaves together, and made themselves aprons." (Gen 3:7).**

This single transgression of God's Law not only brought on the subservience of the soul to the flesh but it also ushered the feared specters of death, Hell and the grave into our world. From this one act of disobedience, man has forever been kept at arms-length from his maker.

Adam's breach of God's Law was so serious that it has been given the appellation of "SIN". And to be clear, God defines SIN thusly: **"sin is the transgression of the law." (1 Jn 3:4)** and **"by the law *is* the knowledge of sin." (Rom 3:20).** Furthermore, as prescribed by the LORD that, **"the wages of sin *is* death;" (Rom 6:23)** each and every person is doomed to death, Hell and the grave if they do not have a Saviour to rescue them from this horrible fate.

Law

Now when the LORD made Adam He gave him a free-will. And with a free-will came the ability to violate God's Law. The LORD God knew this and consequently also endowed man with a conscience.

Because Adam had a conscience, (God's Law written in his heart) ignorance of God's Law could not be used as a defense for his sin. If Adam chose to sin he would be without excuse, his actions would be indefensible.

Coats of Skins

It was via Adam's conscience and God's express commandment that Adam knew that punishment would result from any violation of God's Law.

And so, it is today, doing what you know in your heart is wrong creates a guilty conscience because it is a direct violation of God's Law. The pangs of guilt that result from a guilty conscience are in reality the soul convulsing from an unholy action. The convulsion occurs because the soul knows that God's Law has been violated and that righteous judgment will befall it.

It is very important to realize that without a prescribed punishment, God's Law would, in reality, just be a recommendation. And, no punishment could be warranted or justified for not acting in accordance with a recommendation because, He gave us the free-will or the capacity, to choose what we should do and how we should act.

It should also be pointed out that because God's Law is eternal and unchangeable, death too is eternal and unchangeable. As a side note, there is a huge difference between God's Law and man-made law even though both were established to control man's behavior.

Man-made laws are applied externally to man in an attempt to govern, control, and shape men's actions. It is because man-made laws can only govern physical actions that one can think about performing the most wicked and vile criminal act for a long time and yet never violate the law. Unless an overt violation of a man-made law is committed, there has been no transgression.

In other words, for a violation of the law to be an actual violation, the perpetrator must actualize what they were thinking and commit the violation. This is why law enforcement has to go to great lengths to catch criminals red-handed and no man-made law can legislate morals. Man-made laws at best govern man's social life not their thought life.

God's Law on the other hand, was instilled in man's heart at birth. God's Law is spiritual and works from the heart outward through the physical body into action. It is commonly referred to as our conscience. And because God's Law is spiritual, people's motivations and behaviors cannot be discerned via an autopsy of the physical body.

The Apostle Paul illuminates this truth in *The Epistle of Paul the Apostle to the Romans,* Chapter 2, Verses 14-16:
"For when the Gentiles, which have not the law, do by nature the things contained in the law, thee, having not the law, are a law unto themselves: Which shew the work of the law written in their hearts, their conscience also bearing witness,".

However, contrary to man-made law, when a man decides to transgress God's Law, the violation of the Law takes place. The Scriptures are very clear that, **"the LORD searcheth all hearts, and understandeth all the imaginations of the thoughts:" (1 Chron 28:9).** Or, in other words, the LORD knows and understands your every thought.

Furthermore, the Bible says that if one transgresses God's Law in one point at any time in their life, from birth to death, the man is judged by the LORD to be unrighteous:
"For whosoever shall keep the whole law, and yet offend in one *point*, he is guilty of all." (Jam 2:10).

Now, one must admit, that no mortal has ever been able to even come close to keeping God's Law throughout their entire life. We all know this to be true because every single person has in some way, shape, or form entertained transgressing at least one element of the *Ten Commandments* at some point in their life. Such behavior is inevitable because the soul resides in carnal, lustful flesh. Hence the universal truth that **"all have sinned, and come short of the glory of God;" (Rom 3:23).**

Consequently, it is true, beyond a shadow of a doubt, that every man is unrighteous. Every man is unholy. Every man is a sinner. And, for any who may claim to be *perfect*, may I point out that you are deceived for **"heart *is* deceitful above all *things*, and desperately wicked: who can know it?" (Jer 17:9).**

Fig Leaf Aprons

Upon Adam's commission of sin, his visage instantly became carnal like Eve's. His divine glow instantly ceased. Being aware of this great change in their visage, **"they sewed fig leaves together, and made themselves aprons." (Gen 3:7)** in a vain attempt to hide their unrighteousness from a Thrice-Holy LORD God.

However, because **"eyes of the LORD *are* in every place, beholding the evil and the good." (Prov**

15:3) Adam was found out when the LORD God visited him in the Garden:

"**And they heard the voice of the LORD God walking in the garden in the cool of the day: and Adam and his wife hid themselves from the presence of the LORD God amongst the trees of the garden.**
And the LORD God called unto Adam, and said unto him, Where *art* **thou?**
And the LORD he said, I heard thy voice in the garden, and I was afraid, because I *was* **naked; and I hid myself.**
And he said, Who told thee that thou *wast* **naked? Hast thou eaten of the tree, whereof I commanded thee that thou shouldest not eat?**" **(Gen 3:8-11).**

It was no surprise to Adam that his self-made fig leaf apron could not make him righteous nor cover his sin. Adam fully realized that all his ways were known to the living, all-knowing LORD God. Consequently, we should always keep in mind that no thought or action can be hidden from the LORD.

Adam realized his own fig leaf apron of righteousness was in actuality, just a feeble attempt to try to convince himself that his sins were completely covered and he was still righteous. This can be concluded by the fact that aprons by their very nature only partially cover a person.

Even a cursory look at any kitchen, butcher, or blacksmith apron will verify this fact. Consequently, the most righteous man, the most moral person's self-made fig leaf apron of righteousness can at best only provide the illusion that their sins are covered.

From the day Adam sinned until today, the stubborn fact remains and is attested to in the Scriptures:
"There is a way which seemeth right unto a man, but the end thereof *are* the ways of death." (Prov 14:12).

And, because all mankind was in Adam at the time he sinned, all mankind are born sinners. In other words, because we are all descendants of Adam, we are born unrighteous:
"Behold, I was shapen in iniquity, and in sin did my mother conceive me." (Psm 51:5).

In a word, each and every mortal born into this world is a sinner and must die as payment for being a sinner. Furthermore, one can be sure Adam was afraid of the consequences of his action because he tried to hide from God:

"Adam and his wife hid themselves from the presence of the LORD God amongst the trees of the garden." (Gen 3:8).

Adam knew that **"the LORD thy God, he *is* God, the faithful God, which keepeth covenant and mercy with them that love him and keep his commandments to a thousand generations;
And repayeth them that hate him to their face, to destroy them: he will not be slack to him that hateth him, he will repay him to his face." (Deut 7:9-10).**

Consequently, one can conclude with surety that Adam expected the worst because he knew perfectly well that he was now destined to die.

- Adam knew he was an unrighteous sinner because **"sin is the transgression of the law." (1 Jn 3:4).**

- Adam knew that the body his soul resided in was destined to return to the elements it was created from because the LORD God told him to his face that **"In the sweat of they face shalt thou eat bread, till thou return unto the ground; for out of it wast thou taken: for dust thou *art*, and** unto dust shalt thou return." (Gen 3:19).

- Adam knew his soul was facing eternal damnation because the LORD explicitly stated, **"The soul that sinneth, it shall die" (Ezek 18:20).**

- Adam knew good, (had a past intimate knowledge of good) but was presently intimately and inextricably involved with evil for **"He that committeth sin is of the devil; for the devil sinneth from the beginning." (1 Jn 3:8).**

- Adam knew **"*It is* a fearful thing to fall into the hands of the living God." (Heb 10:31).**

And knowing that only **"righteousness delivereth from death." (Prov 10:2),** Adam, as all men, found himself in an intractable position.

Terror of the LORD

Like King David, Adam must have said:
"My flesh trembleth for fear of thee; and I am afraid of thy judgments." (Psm 119:20). Therefore, Adam most certainly must have searched for something, anything, that he could do to make

himself righteous.

Unfortunately, then as now, man can do **ABSOLUTELY NOTHING** to save himself from the prescribed punishment for sin. What Adam needed was an Emancipator to free him from the Law of Sin and Death. What Adam needed was a Saviour to save him from the penalty of the Law.

Adam was aware that if the punishment for sin was not executed, God could not be a Thrice-Holy and righteous LORD God. He knew full well that God, by his very nature, must judge sin.

In fact, a righteous God could not proclaim a law, pronounce statutes, issue commandments, or expect anyone to walk in His testimonies if He did not judge and punish those who violated them. He knew that **"The LORD, The LORD God, ... will by no means clear *the guilty*;" (Ex 34:6-7)**.

Adam knew that unless he could find a Saviour, he was going to have to face the LORD in judgment and be eternally damned to the Lake of Fire because of his sin.

In all likelihood, the dread and terror he felt was very

similar to that which Job experienced when he met the LORD God face to face, **"For destruction from God was a terror to me, and by reason of his highness I could not endure." (Job 31:23).** So one can conclude that if Job, whom God described as "*a perfect and upright man that feareth God and escheweth evil*" feared greatly, we too should fear the LORD.

Now for those who boast they have "*No Fear*", take note that if you die a sinner and subsequently face the LORD in judgment, you will not only *fear* the LORD, but you will experience the *terror* of the LORD! And terror means just that, <u>TERROR</u>: "*extreme fear, violent dread, fright, fear that agitates the body and mind.*"

It was out of the terror of facing God the Father's full-unabated wrath that Jesus Himself sweated blood asking for another way to pay for mans sin.

Jesus had witnessed firsthand the full wrath of God as He destroyed every living creature except Noah and his family with a worldwide flood, and this is why He prayed:
"Father, if thou be willing, remove this cup from me: nevertheless not my will, but thine, be done.

*****

And being in an agony he prayed more earnestly: and his sweat was as it were great drops of blood falling down to the ground." (Lk 22:42 & 44).

So will you really **"Fear ye not me? saith the LORD: will ye not tremble at my presence, which have placed the sand *for* the bound of the sea by a perpetual decree, that it cannot pass it: and though the waves thereof toss themselves, yet can they not prevail; though they roar, yet can they not pass over it?"** (Jer 5:22).

Adam knew that there is no bargaining with the LORD, because he knew full well that **"God *is* not a man, that he should lie; neither the son of man, that he should repent: hath he said, and shall he not do *it*? or hath he spoken, and shall he not make it good?"** (Num 23:19).

Therefore, Adam knowing the penalty for violating God's law must be paid, he dropped to his knees in Godly sorrow and repented of his sin.

<u>Repentance</u>

Adam repented of his sin upon the full and complete

understanding of his true position with respect to the LORD. Adam repented with Godly sorrow and Godly sorrow worketh repentance unto salvation: **"For godly sorrow worketh repentance to salvation not to be repented of: but the sorrow of the world worketh death." (2 Cor 7:10).**

Godly sorrow and subsequent repentance is brought about when you **"remember your own evil ways, and your doings that *were* not good, and shall loathe yourselves in your own sight for your iniquities and for your abominations." (Ezek 36:31).**

It is only by repentance and faith in the Lord Jesus Christ that the regeneration of your soul (a.k.a. salvation) is possible. Salvation is by repentance and faith and, **"faith *cometh* by hearing, and hearing by the word of God." (Rom 10:17).**

When our Saviour regenerates a person's soul, He performs a divine operation whereby **"he saves us, by the washing of regeneration, and renewing of the Holy Ghost; …" (Titus 3:5).**

A regenerated soul is enlightened to the fact that **"The statutes of the LORD *are* right, rejoicing the**

heart: the commandment of the LORD *is* **pure, enlightening the eyes.**
The fear of the LORD *is* **clean, enduring for ever: the judgments of the LORD** *are* **true** *and* **righteous altogether.**
More to be desired *are they* **than gold, yea, than much fine gold: sweeter also than honey and the honeycomb.**
Moreover by them is thy servant warned: *and* **in keeping of them** *there is* **great reward." (Psm. 19:8-11).**

We know this to be the truth because the LORD God promises **"A new heart also will I give you, and a new spirit will I put within you: and I will take away the stony heart out of your flesh, and I will give you an heart of flesh." (Ezek 36:26).**

For those who doubt the reality of Salvation, consider what the famous English poet, satirist, rake and courtier of King Charles II's Restoration Court John Wilmot, the 2nd Earl of Rochester, told Bishop Burnet regarding his Salvation experience: *"after reading the Scriptures he felt an inward force which did so enlighten his mind and convince him that he could resist it no longer for the words had an authority which did shoot like rays or beams into his mind, so that he was not only convinced by the reasoning he had about it, which satisfied his understanding, but by a power which did so effectually restrain him that he did ever after as firmly believe in his Saviour as if he had seen him in the clouds."* Sadly, while his soul was saved, his flesh paid the full wages of sin. He died in 1680 AD at the age of 33 from venereal disease.

Note well, this spiritual operation can only be performed by the Lord Jesus Christ:
"ye are complete in him, which is the head of all principality and power:
In whom also ye are circumcised with the circumcision made without hands, in putting off the body of the sins of the flesh by the circumcision of Christ:" (Col 2:10-11).

This is because only **"the word of God is quick, and powerful, and sharper than any two-edged sword, piercing even to the dividing asunder of the soul and spirit, and of the joints and marrow, and is a discerner of the thoughts and intents of the heart." (Heb 4:12).**

In addition, take note that the Apostle Paul informs us that until the day of salvation man's heart is veiled with sin:

"**the veil is upon the heart. Nevertheless when it [the soul] shall turn to the Lord, the veil shall be taken away.**" (2 Cor 3:15-16).

Remember that this spiritual operation of cutting away the sin that veils a sinner's heart, can only be performed by the "**sword of the Spirit, which is the word of God:**" **(Eph 6:17)**. And, Jesus Christ is the only one capable of wielding the sword of the Spirit because He was "**declared *to be* the Son of God with power, according to the spirit of holiness, <u>by the resurrection from the dead</u>:**" **(Rom 1:4)**!

Clearly, it is via the process of regeneration "**that our old man is crucified with *him*, that the body of sin might be destroyed, that henceforth we should not serve sin.**
For he that is dead is freed from sin.
Now if we be dead with Christ, we believe that we shall also live with him:
Knowing that Christ being raised from the dead dieth no more; death hath no more dominion over him.
For in that he died, he died unto sin once: but in that he liveth, he liveth unto God.
Likewise reckon ye also yourselves to be dead

indeed unto sin but alive unto God through Jesus Christ our Lord." (Rom 6:6-10).

The author reminds you again, unless your soul is regenerated before you close your eyes in death, you will face God at the Great White Throne Judgment. Don't delude yourself into thinking that day will never come for **"it is appointed unto men once to die, but after this the judgment:" (Heb 9:27)**. And, once judgment has been pronounced, your soul will be damned to eternal suffering in the Lake of Fire *where their worm dieth not and the fire is never quenched!*

As a word to the wise, do not presume upon the Lord because while **"The LORD, The LORD God, [is] merciful and gracious, longsuffering, and abundant in goodness and truth,
Keeping mercy for thousands, forgiving iniquity and transgression and sin, [He] will by no means clear** *the guilty*;**" (Ex 34:6-7).**

Note that the decision to seek the Saviour is yours and yours alone. The choice is totally up to each and every individual because each person is born a free moral agent.

The author earnestly encourages all to choose Jesus Christ as their Saviour **"For in him [Christ] dwelleth all the fullness of the Godhead bodily. And ye are complete in him, which is the head of all principality and power:**

*****

**... wherein also ye are risen with him through the faith of the operation of God, who hath raised him from the dead.
And you, ... hath he quickened together with him, having forgiven you all trespasses;
Blotting out the handwriting of ordinances that was against us, which was contrary to us, and took it out of the way, nailing it to his cross;" (Col 2:9-10, 12-14).**

However, if anyone chooses to disregard the warning, be forewarned that He **"will number you to the sword, and ye shall all bow down to the slaughter: because when I called, ye did not answer; when I spake, ye did not hear; but did evil before mine eyes, and did choose *that* wherein I delighted not." (Isa 65:12).**

Therefore, **"Now be ye not stiffnecked, ... *but* yield yourselves unto the LORD, and enter into his**

sanctuary, which he hath sanctified for ever: and serve the LORD your God, that the fierceness of his wrath may turn away from you." (2 Chron 30:8).

"For if they escaped not who refused him that spake on earth, much more *shall not* we *escape*, if we turn away from him that *speaketh* from heaven:" (Heb 12:25).

<u>Mercy</u>

Hearing Adam's heartfelt plea, the LORD extended mercy because **"He looketh upon men, and *if any* say, I have sinned, and perverted *that which was* right, and it profited me not;
He will deliver his soul from going into the pit, and his life shall see the light." (Job 33:27-28).**

The LORD God extended mercy to Adam because the Lord; **"knoweth our frame; he remembereth that we are dust." (Psm 103:14).** It was only because the LORD is a gracious and merciful God that He did not utterly consume Adam and Eve, or forsake them.

With his prayer answered, Adam rejoiced, as all the

saved also proclaim **"I will praise thee, O Lord my God, with all my heart: and I will glorify thy name for evermore. For great *is* thy mercy toward me: and thou hast delivered my soul from the lowest hell." (Psm 86:12-13).**

All should be very thankful that **"The LORD taketh pleasure in them that fear him, in those that hope in his mercy." (Psm 147:11).** Jesus confirmed God's mercy for man when He declared, **"I came not to call the righteous, but sinners to repentance." (Lk 5:32).**

It is due only to God's mercy that **"God hast punished us less than our iniquities *deserve*, and hast given us *such* deliverance as this [salvation]" (Ezra 9:13).** In fact, all should realize that it is only by the grace of God that all unregenerated souls are not currently burning in Hell this very moment.

It is only because **"The LORD is ... longsuffering to us-ward, not willing that any should perish, but that all should come to repentance." (2 Pet 3:9)** that He has given mankind another day to repent and seek salvation.

It was only because Adam acknowledged his own

futile attempt at righteousness and repented of his sin, that the LORD extended mercy. It was due to Adam's repentance that the LORD informed Adam that He **"hath put away thy sin, thou shalt not die." (2 Sam 12:13).**

It was through the making of the coats of skins whereby Adam was to learn that it is only **"By mercy and truth iniquity is purged:" (Prov 16:6).**

It was through the making of the coats of skins whereby Adam was to learn that **"In the fear of the LORD *is* strong confidence: and his children shall have a place of refuge." (Prov 14:26).**

It was through the making of the coats of skins that Adam was to learn that **"As he came forth of his mother's womb, naked shall he return to go as he came, and shall take nothing of his labor, which he may carry away in his hand." (Ecc 5:15).**

It was through the making of the coats of skins that Adam and Eve learned **"*It is of* the LORD's mercies that we are not consumed, because his compassions fail not.
They are new every morning: great *is* thy faithfulness." (Lam 2:22-23).**

It was through the making of coats of skins, that Adam and Eve were soon to be able to rejoice and say, **"he hath clothed me with the garments of salvation, he hath covered me with the robe of righteousness," (Isa 61:10).**

Step 1. The Altar

With God's mercy extended the author believes that the LORD instructed Adam to construct **"An altar of earth thou shalt make unto me, and shalt sacrifice thereon thy burnt offerings," (Ex 20:24).**

The first order of business for Adam was to build an altar whereby he could make the required blood sacrifice for his sin. It needed to be a blood sacrifice because **"without shedding of blood is no remission [of sin]." (Heb 9:22).**

The altar was most likely 3 cubits high, and 5 cubits foursquare (7.5 feet wide, 7.5 feet long, 4.5 feet high) based upon the dimensions of the Brazen Altar:
"the altar of burnt offering of shittim wood: five cubits was the length thereof, and five cubits the breadth thereof; it was foursquare; and three cubits the height thereof." (Ex. 38:1).

Now, if one examines the numerological aspects of the altar's volume one notices that the Altar of Burnt Offerings would have been 75 cubic cubits. The number 75 is the multiplicative product of its mathematical factors, 3 and 5. The number 3 is the first *prime* number and is found throughout the Bible.

Being a *prime* number, it is indivisible by anything other and 1 and itself. Consequently, the number 3 represents the one and only LORD God, which is a triune Deity.

It is important to understand that **"God *is* a Spirit:" (Jn 4:24)** and is comprised of a threefold personality existing of three infinite coequal and co-eternal persons. Furthermore, one should note that one of the *prime* attributes of the Trinity is that He is indivisible: **"the Father, the Word, and the Holy Ghost: and these three are one." (1 Jn 5:7).**

In addition, by 3 being a *prime* number it expresses the true and primary definition of something, namely; the causal agent for an action, (i.e. the *prime* cause). Hence, the number 3 in Scripture always represents the fact that God was the *prime* causal agent behind an event or action because when God does something

"nothing can be put to it, nor any thing taken from it: and God doth *it*, that *men* should fear before him." (Ecc 3:14).

Case in point, Jesus Christ rose bodily from the grave on the 3rd day indicating that this was not a natural event but one performed under the auspices of God.

"Moreover brethren, I declare unto you the gospel which I preached unto you, which also ye have received, and wherein ye stand;
By which also ye are saved, …
Christ died for our sins according to the scriptures;
And that he was buried, and that he rose again the third day according to the scriptures:" (1 Cor 15:1-4).

Jesus resurrected on the 3rd day because He was righteous. He knew no sin and no sin was found in Him. Consequently, death had no hold on him. This is clearly verified in the Scriptures.

"I lay down my life, that I might take it again. No man taketh it from me, but I lay it down of myself. I have power to lay it down, and I have power to take it again. This commandment have I received of my Father." (Jn 10:17-18).

The number 5 is also a *prime* number and is universally acknowledged to represent God's grace and mercy. The number 5, like 3, is indivisible by anything other than 1 and itself, and being a *prime* number, reinforces the fact that grace and mercy are neither composites nor derivatives of anything but are *prime* attributes of the LORD.

These attributes are why the Apostle Paul's advised that the regenerated look **"unto Jesus the author and finisher of *our* faith; who for the joy that was set before him endured the cross, despising the shame, and is set down at the right hand of the throne of God.**
For consider him that endured such contradiction of sinners against himself, lest ye be wearied and faint in your minds." (Heb 12:2-3).

Who can fully comprehend why **"God commendeth his love toward us, in that, while we were yet sinners, Christ died for us." (Rom 5:8)**? And why **"That in the ages to come he might shew the exceeding riches of his grace in *his* kindness toward us through Christ Jesus." (Eph 2: 7).**

Adam then leveled the 75 cubic cubit alter of earth

into a 3 cubit high, perfectly flat, horizontal weight-bearing surface. This would have been a sizable undertaking for a single person to perform but served to illustrate the exacting nature of a righteous LORD.

One should take special notice of what a blessing it is that the altar was just 3 cubits above ground level. This height illustrates that a *prime* attribute of the atonement Jesus Christ made for sin is that it is within easy reach of all men.

Because **"The LORD *is* a man of war:" (Ex 15:3)** an elevated altar was a necessity from a military standpoint. An elevated altar illustrated that one needs to rise above the world in order to espy the approach of the Devil; **"your adversary the devil, as a roaring lion, walketh about, seeding whom he may devour:" (2 Pet 5:8)**.

Believe it or not, there is a spiritual battle going on over the souls of men and those on the Lord's side are the only ones who can acclaim, **"The LORD *is* my rock, and my fortress, and my deliverer; my god, my strength, in whom I will trust; my buckler, and the horn of my salvation, *and* my high tower.
I will call upon the LORD, *who is worthy* to be praised: so shall I be saved from mine enemies."**

(Psm 18:2-3).

Another reason the altar was elevated above ground level was to get above the earth's atmospheric boundary layer. The wind is subject to unpredictable turbulence and eddy currents up to an elevation of approximately 3 feet above the ground.

However, from approximately 3 feet upward one enjoys the steady prevailing morning and afternoon breezes. This is why older homes were built with the first floor and porches elevated about 3 feet above ground level.

Furthermore, the altar being in the prevailing breezes foreshadowed the comings and goings of the Holy Spirit as Jesus explained to Nicodemus, **"Marvel not that I said unto thee, Ye must be born again. The wind bloweth where it listeth, and thou hearest the sound thereof, but canst not tell whence it cometh, and whither it goeth: so is every one that is born of the Spirit." (Jn 3:7-8).**

Therefore, being above worldly influences **"we which are alive *and* remain shall be caught up together with them in the clouds, to meet the Lord in the air: and so shall we ever be with the Lord.**

Wherefore comfort one another with these words." (1 Thes 4:17-18).

Additionally, the altar needed to be elevated to illustrate that the LORD's ways are above man's comprehension and above finding out:
"*as* **the heavens are higher than the earth, so are my ways higher than your ways, and my thoughts than your thoughts.**" (Isa 55:9),
and the Lord "**giveth not account of any of his matters.**" (Job 33:13).

So, remember we can rely on God's promise of resurrection and escape from eternal damnation in the Lake of Fire because, "**God** *is* **not a man, that he should lie; neither the son of man, that he should repent: hath he said, and shall he not do** *it*? **or hath he spoken, and shall he not make it good?**" **(Num 23:19).**
It is also important to note that the LORD forbid any steps leading up to the altar:
"**Neither shalt thou go up by steps unto mine altar, that thy nakedness be not discovered thereon.**" **(Ex 20:26)**
thereby precluding any steps man may think he needs to take in order for his sacrifice to be acceptable to God.

This command points out that the sacrifice, when performed as prescribed by the LORD, is sufficient. Nothing needs to be added to it. Nothing needs to be taken from it.

Any steps taken by man are forbidden and will only serve to elevate man in the eyes of men. And, such religious self-aggrandizement is warned against, because instead of assisting, in actuality, it voids their sin offering.

Not only that, but such religious self-aggrandizement showcases the fig leaf apron that the person is wearing. It showcases that the person is actually naked and unrighteous. Consequently, trying to assist Jesus Christ with His payment for our sin such as, doing good works, giving to religious organizations, penance, asceticism, self-mutilation, baptisms, etc. avails absolutely nothing.

Heed the warning, all that attempt to add to Jesus Christ's self-sacrifice, need to take a step back, and realize that to the LORD, **"all our righteousness are as filthy rags;" (Isa 64:6).**

The bottom line is, there are no steps any man can

take to earn, facilitate, or be owed salvation. Do not ever forget it is **"by grace are ye saved through faith; <u>and that not of yourselves</u>:** *it is* **the gift of God: <u>Not of works, lest any man should boast.</u>" (Eph 2:8-9).**

The altar being four square is also significant from a numerological standpoint. The number 4 represents the number for the world. It is also the first number that is divisible, and as all know, the world is certainly divided.

The multiple elements that make up the world have been proven to be sub-dividable and this is the entire aim and purpose of Materials Science. In addition, as all mortals know, the world breaks down not only into physical elements but also into choices: (i.e. good vs. evil, right vs. wrong, believe the Bible vs. do not believe the Bible).

Please, do not ever lose sight of the fact that **"wide** *is* **the gate, and broad** *is* **the way, that leadeth to destruction, and many there be which go in thereat:**
Because strait *is* **the gate, and narrow** *is* **the way, which leadeth unto life, and few there be that find it." (Mat 7:13-14).**

A square also illustrates the point that God has set definite limits or boundaries upon mankind. His grace and long-suffering extends only so far: **"Behold, he cometh with clouds; and every eye shall see him, and they *also* which pierced him: and all kindreds of the earth shall wail because of him." (Rev 1:6).**

One should also note that the number 4 is not a prime number hence the LORD God does **not** provide His reinforcement of authority for unregenerated man's behavior on earth.

Unregenerated man definitely does **not** behave as sanctioned by the LORD God. In fact, **"God is angry *with the wicked* every day." (Psm 7:11) "because ye have sinned against the LORD, and have not obeyed the voice of the LORD, nor walked in his law, nor in his statutes, nor in his testimonies; therefore this evil is happened unto you, as at this day." (Jer 44:23).**

The number 4 also speaks of the directions of the earth (North, South, East, West) hence the square cross section of the altar illustrated that God can be found no matter where on earth you live. And it

illustrated that the altar is approachable from any direction in life a person may have trod.
"For the hope which is laid up for you in heaven, whereof ye heard before in the word of the truth of the gospel; Which is come unto you, as *it is* **in all the world;" (Col 1:5-6).**

Additionally, the number 4 also speaks to worldly divisions such as the Seasons (Spring, Summer, Autumn, Winter) and Days (Morning, Afternoon, Evening, Night), etc. The spiritual lesson is the **"LORD, make me to know mine end, and the measure of my days, what it** *is***;** *that* **I may know how frail I** *am***." (Psm 39:4).**

Step 2. Firewood

With the altar complete, Adam loaded it with firewood. The author believes God directed Adam to cut down the very fig tree he had used to make his fig leaf apron.

In the *Gospel According to Luke*, Jesus **"... spake also this parable; A certain** *man* **had a fig tree planted in his vineyard; and he came and sought fruit thereon, and found none.**
Then said he unto the dresser of the vineyard,

**Behold, these three years I come seeking fruit on this fig tree, and find none: cut it down; why cumbereth it the ground?
And he answering said unto him, Lord, let it alone this year also, till I shall dig about it, and dung it: And if it bear fruit, *well*: and if not, *then* after that thou shalt cut it down." (Lk 13:6-9).**

Cutting down the fig tree would have served to illustrate, as the above parable shows, that God expects all men to bear fruit and **"the fruit of the Spirit is love, joy, peace, longsuffering, gentleness, goodness, faith,
Meekness, temperance: against such there is no law. And they that are Christ's have crucified the flesh with the affections and lusts." (Gal 5:22-24).**

Men are not to use the natural things of this world as an excuse for unrighteousness. Furthermore, spiritual fruit can only come from a righteous soul for **"Doth a fountain send forth at the same place sweet *water* and bitter?
Can the fig tree, by brethren, bear olive berries? either a vine, figs? so *can* no fountain both yield salt water and fresh." (Jam 3:11-12).**

However, if the fig tree fails to produce fruit, if the

unregenerate refuses to repent of their sins and ask the Lord to regenerate their soul, they will be cast into the Lake of Fire for **"If a man abide not in me [Jesus], he is cast forth as a branch, and is withered; and men gather *them* into the fire, and they are burned." (Jn 15:6).**

The lesson for Adam was that had he not repented he would have faced the full-unabated fiery wrath of the LORD God and would have been totally consumed: **"But the wicked shall perish, and the enemies of the LORD *shall be* as the fat of lambs: they shall consume; into smoke shall they consume away" (Psm 37:20).**

Be forewarned:

"the LORD thy God *is* a consuming fire, *even* a jealous God." (Deut 4:24).

"And now also the axe is laid unto the root of the trees: therefore every tree which bringeth not forth good fruit is hewn down, and cast into the fire." (Mat 3:10).

This simple yet clear reminder to Adam was that sinful man shall meet his maker:
"For it is written, *As* I live, saith the Lord, every

knee shall bow to me, and every tongue shall confess to God.
So then every one of us shall give account of himself to God." (Rom 14:11-12).

Step 3. The Sacrifice

With the altar ready for a sacrifice, Adam pondered what he should lay on it to atone for his sin. This same quandary faces all who take the long view of life.

In years gone by heathens sacrificed their first-born child. Others believe "*good works*", penance, or alms will be adequate. However, no matter what one lays on the altar of their god there persists the nagging question of assurance:

- How can I know for certain that my sacrifice was sufficient?

- What happens if my sacrifice when weighed in the eternal scale of righteousness is found to be wanting?

These question of how your belief system deals with the atonement of your sin is of the upmost importance because the very next event after physical death is the

judgment:
"for it is appointed unto men once to die, but after this the judgement." (Heb 9:27).

So, how does one atone for their transgressions? Unfortunately, the truth is, no person can atone for their own transgressions. What all need is someone with the wherewithal to mediate a permanent reconciliation with God the Father by atoning for all transgressions.

Thankfully the inerrant Holy Scriptures identify the only one capable of serving as such a mediator by name. This named mediator is none other than the God-man Jesus Christ. He is mankind's only Saviour because only He is capable of emancipating all from sin and saving all from the Law of Sin and Death. **"there is one God, and one mediator between God and men, the man Christ Jesus." (1 Tim 2:5).**

Without The Saviour, you will face judgment as a sinner because you died with an unrighteous, unregenerated soul. You died in your sins. There is no other way to put it other than ***you died a sinner*** and must face God Almighty and receive the punishment for sin.

Adam knew **"it *is* the blood *that* maketh an atonement for the soul." (Lev 17:11).** He also knew that for the atonement to be acceptable to God, the person whose life was to be sacrificed, the person whose blood was to be shed as payment for mans sin, had to be **"a male without blemish" (Lev 1:3).**

The person had to be a male and had to be perfect and Adam like all of his descendants are nowhere near perfect. Consequently, the question before Adam was, how was he to find a perfect, sinless person that would be willing to voluntarily sacrifice his own life for his sin?

Thankfully, before the foundation of the world God knew that His Son would be willing to be that perfect sinless person. God would in the fullness of time send his only begotten Son, Jesus Christ to be the required sacrifice for mankind's sin. And as incontestable proof of his perfection and sinlessness he arose from the dead on the third day proving beyond a shadow of a doubt that **"in him was life" (Jn 1:4)!**

It is important to note that no mortal man could ever be an acceptable sacrifice. The blood sacrifice must be perfect, that is to say, righteous, sinless, without blame. And, we know that among mortal men **"There is none righteous, no not one: There is none that understandeth, there is none that seeketh after God. They are all gone out of the way, they are together become unprofitable; there is none that doeth good, no not one." (Rom 3:10-12)**.

Because no mortal man could ever qualify as an acceptable sacrifice, God instructed Adam that physically perfect animals were to be substitute sacrifices until such time, that Jesus Christ, a truly perfect man, a truly righteous man, a truly sinless man would come along. Until then, animals were to serve as a reminder that sin needs to be dealt with before one dies because with the **"*sacrifices there is a remembrance again *made* of sins every year.*" (Heb 10:4)**.

One reason animals were the prescribed substitute sacrifice was that they could be inspected for physical perfection illustrating that man's Saviour would be perfect. Also, physically perfect animals are relatively easy to obtain and, because animals cannot sin because they do not have souls, the requirement that the sacrifice be sinless was satisfied.

In addition to being perfect, righteous, and sinless, the man must also willing volunteer to be the sacrifice for our sins. He would have to volunteer to be the sacrifice because He Himself being righteous and sinless, would have no reason to perform any sacrifice at all much less serve as the sacrifice for the sins of others.

Down through the ages men were constantly reminded that **"*it is* not possible that the blood of bulls and of goats should take away sins." (Heb 10:4)** and all should always be looking for the coming of the Messiah who would be the **"propitiation [complete, perfect, and total payment] for our sins: and not for ours only, but also for *the sins* of the whole world." (1 Jn 2:2).**

What God's law demanded, and what all men need is an innocent, perfect, righteous, sacrifice to atone for their sin. Thankfully, in the fullness of time Jesus Christ, the Son of God, the God-man Christ Jesus, stood in the gap and voluntarily sacrificed Himself.

The Saviour came born of a woman, and **"put away sin by the sacrifice of himself." (Heb 9:26).** He voluntarily sacrificed himself to atone for our sin. It is because Jesus Christ was the fully accepted sacrifice for man's sin that *"there is* **no more offering for sin." (Heb 10:18)** required.

This fact is highly significant and serves as yet another verification of His divinity because, **"scarcely for a righteous man will one die: yet peradventure for a good man some would even dare to die.
But God commendeth his love toward us, in that, while we were yet sinners, Christ died for us." (Rom 5:7-8).**

Indeed, Adam knew the LORD **"hast in love to my soul** *delivered it* **from the pit of corruption: for thou hast cast all my sins behind thy back." (Isa 38:17).**

Indeed, Adam most certainly realized that, thanks to Christ Jesus, **"I am escaped with the skin of my teeth." (Job 19:20)**.

Indeed, Adam knew that the coming Saviour was **"the way, the truth, and the life: [and] no man cometh unto the Father, but by [him]." (Jn 14:6).**

The author strongly advises all to take a lesson from practical life experiences. Once you enter the courtroom in judgment, it is too late to make amends. Jesus Christ is the only one who can fulfill the requirement of atoning for your sins. We know this is an absolute truth because Jesus stated **"I am the resurrection, and the life: he that believeth in, though he were dead, yet shall live." (Jn 11:25)**. Can anything be more clear?

May I also point out that the 1611 King James Bible is the only book in the entire universe of literature that says: ***Thus saith the LORD***. So, the author asks you again, what does the book you place your trust in say? What will your god do about your sin and, what is the proof?

Step 4. Slaying

With Adam humbly standing before the Altar of Burnt Offerings the LORD commanded that an animal sacrifices be made until such time that He would send His Son to be the propitiation for sin.

Animal sacrifices were to be performed as a continual reminder of mankind's sinfulness and need of salvation. The sacrifice's bloodshed, would serve to enforce the Divine decree that **"without shedding of blood is no remission [of sin]." (Heb 9:22)** for **"it *is*** the blood *that* maketh an atonement for the soul." (Lev 17:11).

We can be confident that a ram was selected animal because *The Book of Proverbs*, Chapter 27, Verse 26 informs us "**The lambs *are* for thy clothing,**".

Additionally, the tabernacle roof was constructed of rams skins; "**thou shalt make a covering for the tent *of* rams' skins dyed red,**" (Ex 26:14) indicating that the Lamb of God's shed blood would shield man from God's wrath and provide a way to come unto the Throne of God. Jesus' shed blood would shield and provide protection from the Devil, the "**prince of the power of the air**" (Eph 2:1).

With Adam standing face to face with his substitute. He was instructed to look it straight in the eyes, and lay both his hands on its head to fully and unequivocally acknowledge that this poor innocent animal was going to give its life for his sin. For Adam's personal transgression of God's Law, "**he shall put his hand upon the head of the burnt offering; and it shall be accepted for him to make atonement for him.**" (Lev 1:4).

With a razor-sharp knife in hand, Adam slit the ram's

throat from ear to ear;
"he shall kill the ram before the LORD:" (Lev 1:5).

While painless if properly done because the animal instantly loses consciousness due to the sudden drop in blood pressure, this act was still horrific because this was the first ever shedding of blood. This slaying was the very first death in what formally was a perfect world.

Adam plunged the knife into the ram's neck, and this poor innocent animal, with blood spurting from the severed carotid arteries and its eyes still riveted upon Adam's eyes, slumped to the ground, limp and lifeless at Adam's feet as its last breath of life whistled out through its violated trachea.

Adam witnessed firsthand the heart-rending experience of seeing the light of life fade out of the ram's eyes into the stillness and irreversibility of death. This slaying graphically illustrated that the penalty for sin is most certainly death, and death is a very heart-rending experience to witness.

One can only imagine that at the first sight of this bloody spectacle, Adam must have experienced the same vertigo and nausea that everyone experiences the first time they witness a person's bloody demise.

Furthermore, such an event is unforgettable and the events and emotions surrounding it are indelibly etched in one's mind. Recollections of which continually resurface and haunt one's conscience until the day of death, hence the warning:
"Be ye afraid of the sword: for wrath *bringeth* the punishments of the sword, that ye may know *there is* a judgment" (Job 19:29).

One should also remember this was not just any old ram. This ram was not some sort of a wild, savage beast. This ram was completely tame and docile. It was completely submissive to Adam's authority.

Most likely this ram was the very same animal that God brought before Adam to name:
**"And out of the ground the LORD God formed every best of the field, and every fowl of the air; and brought *them* unto Adam to see what he would call them: and whatsoever Adam called every living creature, that was the name thereof.
And Adam gave names to all cattle, and to the fowl of the air, and to every beast of the field; ..." (Gen 2:19-20).**

God Himself had given Adam dominion over all the cattle and over all the earth and now Adam had killed what God had put under his authority and protection. What a horrific and gut-wrenching experience this must have been for Adam. But then on the other hand think how God felt when His creation, made in His own image, knowingly rebelled by choosing to know evil instead of being content with just knowing good.

Thanks be to God that He had mercy on us sinners. What a blessing that **"we are sanctified through the offering of the body of Jesus Christ once *for all*." (Heb 10:10).**

Thankfully, **"For by one offering he [Jesus Christ] hath perfected for ever them that are sanctified." (Heb 10:14), "And their sins and iniquities will I [the Lord] remember no more." (Heb 10:18).**

Step 5. Blood Applied

As the blood spurted out of the ram's neck, Adam collected some of it and sprinkled it around and upon the altar:
"and sprinkle the blood round about upon the altar" (Lev 1:5).

Adam sprinkled the blood on the top, sides, and base of the altar indicating that there can be no access to God, from any direction, save through the shed blood of our Saviour, the LORD Jesus Christ.

Remember:
"Jesus saith unto him, I am the way, the truth, and the life: no man cometh unto the Father, but by me." (Jn 14:6).

The blood sprinkled round about upon the altar foreshadowed **"Jesus the mediator of the new covenant, and to the blood of sprinkling, that speaketh better things than *that of* Abel." (Heb 12:24)** and reinforced the incontrovertible fact that man can only be; **"made nigh [to God] by the blood of Christ" (Eph 2:13)**.

Jesus' self-sacrifice is why the saints in Glory proclaim that Jesus **"art worthy to take the book, and to open the seals thereof: for thou wast slain, and hast redeemed us to God by thy blood out of every kindred, and tongue, and people, and nation;**
And hast made us unto our God kings and priests: and we shall reign on the earth." (Rev 5:9-10).

Step 6. Flaying

Once the ram had been slain, it was flayed:
"he shall flay the burnt offering" (Lev 1:6),.

Flaying indicated that Jesus laid aside His glory and **"made himself of no reputation, and took upon him the form of a servant, and was made in the likeness of men:" (Phil 2:7).**

God has absolutely no use for willful flesh because it was the lusts of the flesh that Adam's soul yielded to, and by yielding to them, he brought a curse upon all mankind and the world. There is no question about it, **"No flesh should glory in his presence." (1 Cor 1:29).**

Flaying also made the point that willful flesh is separated from God:
"your iniquities have separated between you and your God and your sins have hid *his* face from you, that he will not hear." (Isa 59:2).

Additionally. it highlighted the fact that the flesh has no intrinsic life within itself, but is useful to man, **only** if he knows how to make it conform to his will.

Coats of Skins

Likewise, salvation of the soul has no profit for the flesh;
"It is the spirit that quickeneth; the flesh profiteth nothing" (Jn 6:63).

It is interesting to note that the outermost layer of the tabernacle's roof was made of badger skins; **"thou shalt make a covering for the tent *of* rams' skins dyed red, and a covering above *of* badgers' skins." (Ex 26:14).**

This indicated that the Lord Jesus Christ **"hath no form nor comeliness; and when we shall see him, *there is* no beauty that we should desire him." (Isa 52:2).** And, as anyone who has visited a furrier can attest, badger skin coats are not a commercial commodity. There are seal, bear, beaver, fox, raccoon, rabbit, mink, and chinchilla fur coats but one will never find a badger skin coat hanging on the rack.

Jesus came in the **likeness** of sinful flesh and badgers are a perfect parallel for the flesh because badgers are vicious, carnivorous, grizzled-gray little animals with very little redeeming attributes, just like sinful man.

It is interesting to note however that they do have a

white streak on their head indicating, that like man there exists a possibility of being washed white as snow.

Therefore:
"Come now, and let us reason together, saith the LORD: though your sins be as scarlet, they shall be white as snow; thought they be red like crimson, they shall be as wool." (Isa 1:18).

Flaying also served as a reminder that *"the LORD seeth* **not as man seeth; for man looketh on the outward appearance, but the LORD looketh on the heart." (1Sam 16:7).** Flaying showed that man should not exclusively look at the human-side, of Christ.

It is without argument that Jesus was a great philosopher, a great prophet, a great man, and a great example of how man was to live amongst their fellow man. However, we are not to look towards the outward man, but to view Jesus as John the Baptist saw him:

"Behold the Lamb of God, which taketh away the sin of the world." (Jn 1:29), "whose shoe's latchet I am not worthy to unloose." (Jn 1:27).

This operation illustrated that man needs to look

beyond the earthly life of Jesus and see who the man Christ Jesus truly is, the **"one mediator between God and men, Who gave himself a ransom for all" (1 Tim 2:5-6).**

Step 7. Field Dressing

The flayed hide was then field-dressed to preserve it until it could be tanned and used to make the coats of skins.

Field dressing the hide was accomplished by stretching the hide out and staking it to the ground, inner-side up. After staking, the hide was thoroughly scraped to remove as much subcutaneous fat as possible.

This operation was performed immediately after flaying, while the hide was still warm, because once the hide cooled, fat removal became much more problematic. This staking and hide scraping illustrated to Adam that trusting in the flesh, pins one down to a cursed world and sooner or later your body will be separated from its accumulation of worldly possessions.

Staking the hide to the ground clearly illustrated that

sinful flesh would never enter the realms of Glory but is forever earthbound because **"for dust thou *art*, and unto dust shalt thou return." (Gen 3:19).**

Adam learned too late that God was not kidding when He said **"Cursed be the man that obeyeth not the words of his covenant," (Jer 11:3).**

Now, an animal's subcutaneous fat that surrounds the body represents the accumulated physical possessions we surround ourselves with. It is this subcutaneous fat that gives an animal's coat that rich a rich and luxurious rippling sheen.

And so it is with man. A plethora of possessions give one the appearance of richness but we are warned that being rich in faith is much more to be desired for **"Happy is the man that findeth wisdom, and the man that getteth understanding. For the merchandise of it is better than the merchandise of silver, and the gain thereof than fine gold. She is more precious than rubies: and all the things thou canst desire are not to be compared unto her." (Prov 3:13-15).**

It is the **"Blessing of the LORD, it maketh rich, and he addeth no sorrow with it." (Prov 10:22).**

Too much fat also inhibits useful action. Too much materialism actually becomes a hindrance so **"Take heed, and beware of covetousness: for a mans life consisteth not in the abundance of things which he possesseth." (Lk 12:15).**

Placing the subcutaneous fat atop of the firewood on the altar served to inform Adam that when the LORD returns, everything man has, everything man holds dear, and everything man places any sort of value on, shall be totally destroyed by fire:
"the day of the LORD will come as a thief in the night; in the which the heavens shall pass away with a great noise, and the elements shall melt with fervent heat, the earth also and the works that are therein shall be burned up.
Seeing **then** *that* **all these things shall be dissolved, what manner** *of persons* **ought ye to be in** *all* **holy conversation and godliness,**
Looking for and hasting unto the coming of the day of God, wherein the heavens being on fire shall be dissolved, and the elements shall melt with fervent heat?" (2 Pet 3:10-12).

Another point for consideration was that an animal without any fat at all is by definition, a lean animal.

By Adam partaking of the fruit of the tree of the knowledge of good and evil in order to have his **"eyes opened, and to be as gods, knowing good and evil" (Gen 3:5)**, he forsook the mercy of God and God **"gave them their request; but sent leanness into their soul." (Psm 106:15).**

The lesson for all that followed Adam was, that forsaking God brings limitations, want, and death, not blessings:
"Thus saith the LORD; Cursed be the man that trusteth in man, and maketh flesh his arm, and whose heart departeth from the LORD." (Jer 15:5).

It is because Adam did not walk by faith, that the LORD God made the pronouncement:
"cursed *is* the ground for thy sake; in sorrow shalt not eat *of* it all the days of thy life;
Thorns also and thistles shall it bring forth to thee; and thou shalt eat the herb of the field;
In the sweat of thy face shalt thou eat bread, till thou return unto the ground; for out of it was thou taken; for dust thou *art*, and unto dust shalt thou return." (Gen 3:17-19).

Note that it is important that the hide should be field dressed while still warm. Salvation too, is much more readily accomplished if one's heart has been warmed by hearing the good news of the Gospel.

And just like field dressing a cold hide, getting a cold-hearted person to see themselves as God sees them, and making them realize that they owe all to Him, is much more difficult, and the accomplishment of a true salvation experience is much less likely.

Remember, it was for man's sake that the LORD cursed the ground. It was for man's sake that **"in sorrow shalt thou eat *of* it [the ground] all the days of thy life." (Gen 3:17).**

Why was this a blessing for man? The answer is found in the old axiom, *idle hands are the Devil's workshop*. It is the woes of this world that drive us to seek our Saviour. It is only the Gospel of Christ that **"brings glad tidings of good things!" (Rom 10:15).**

Step 8. Salting

The next order of business was for Adam to salt the field-dressed hide. Salting prevented putrefaction of the collagen during the time between flaying and tanning.

What clearer picture of how the Gospel of Christ, which is the power of God unto salvation of your soul, preserves a soul unto eternal life could be possible?

The world is unforgiving and harsh and man is born into it unsalted, a sinner:

"*As for* thy [the unsaved, unregenerated soul's] nativity, in the day thou wast born thy navel was not cut, neither wast thou washed in water to supple *thee;* thou wast not salted at all, nor swaddled at all.
None eye pitied thee, to do any of these unto thee, to have compassion upon thee; but thou was cast out in the open field, to the loathing of thy person, in the day that thou wast born." (Ezek 16:4-5).

Washing newborn infants in a dilute saline solution not only served to cleanse and disinfect the newborn but it also testified of the need of salvation for every man born of a woman.

In *The Gospel According to Matthew,* Chapter 5, Verse 13 the Apostle Matthew makes it very clear that

"Ye [all regenerated souls] are the salt of the earth:".

Because Christians have the indwelling of the Spirit of Holiness, they are the earth's preserving element that is staving off the judgment of God:
**"For the mystery of iniquity doth already work: only he [God] who now letteth will let, until he [Holy Spirit] be taken out of the way.
And then shall the Wicked be revealed, whom the Lord shall consume with the spirit of his mouth, and shall destroy with the brightness of his coming." (2 Thes 2:7-8).**

Until then, our speech is to *"be* **alway with grace, seasoned with salt," (Col 4:6).**

Remember:
"Salt *is* **good: but if the salt have lost his savour, wherewith shall it be seasoned.
It is neither fit for the land, nor yet for the dunghill;** *but* **men cast it out. He that hath ears to hear, let him hear." (Lk 14:34-35).**

Salting required that Adam rub generous amount of salt into the hide. He was careful to ensure that the entire inner surface was treated and that the salt was worked well down into the hide thereby preserving it and keeping it from corrupting.

He then thoroughly air-dried the hide and after 3 days, scraped off the saturated salt.

One should also note that the salt was left on for 3 days, which attests to the fact that the LORD is the *prime* causal agent of salvation. In addition, it foreshadowed the fact that Jesus would rise bodily from the dead after three days in the tomb as verifiable proof that **"In him was life;" (Jn 1:4)** and **"whosoever believeth in him shall receive remission of sins." (Acts 10:43).**

Jesus was sinless, he was salt through and through. In fact, Jesus said **"I am the way, the truth, and the life: no man cometh unto the Father, but by me."** because **"In him was life; and the life was the light of men." (Jn 1:4).**

He is the WAY that leads to God the Father via His doctrine, His example, His self-sacrifice and by His Spirit.

He is the TRUTH that teaches the knowledge of God and directs in the way in opposition to all false religions. He enlightens us to all the promises of God and to the purpose of the Mosaic Law which was only the shadow and not the truth or substance of the good things which were to come.

He is the LIFE that animates all those who seek and serve Him and will not only save from death but destroys it whereby His grace and glory will be enjoyed eternally at the end of the way.

Step 9. Dissection

Setting aside the salted hide, Adam then took the skinned ram and meticulously dissected it. Each inward element was washed, and closely examined.

Adam was instructed to **"cut it into his pieces.
And ... shall put fire upon the altar, and lay the wood in order upon the fire:
And ... lay the parts, the head, and the fat, in order upon the wood that** *is* **on the fire which** *is* **upon the altar:
But his inwards and his legs shall he wash in water: and the priest shall burn all on the altar,** *to be* **a burnt sacrifice, an offering made by fire, of a sweet savour unto the LORD." (Lev 1:6-9)**.

Closely examining the dissected animal served to illustrate that no matter how closely anyone examines our Saviour, Jesus Christ, they will find no sin. He is our perfect sin offering because He was **"without sin" (Heb 4:15)**.

People have tried for centuries to find fault with Jesus Christ but no one has been able to find one single imperfection. Christ threw down the gauntlet prior to his crucifixion with the challenge **"Which of you convinceth me of sin?" (Jn 8:46)** and 2018 years later, while many have tried, not one single person has succeeded.

So, before you decide to dismiss Jesus Christ as nothing more than a mythical person who allegedly performed a few miracles, consider well the warning: **"Woe unto him that striveth with his Maker! … Shall the clay say to him that fashioneth it, What makest thou?" (Isa 45:9).**

Washing each element in water served to show that Christ was filled with the Spirit of Holiness **"For in him dwelleth all the fullness of the Godhead bodily." (Col 2:9).**

The washing of the inwards and legs verified that our

sacrifice for sin, Jesus Christ"
"being in the form of God, thought it not robbery to be equal with God:
But made himself of no reputation, and took upon him the form of a servant, and was made in the likeness of men:
And being found in fashion as a man, he humbled himself, and became obedient unto death, even the death of the cross." (Phil 2:6-8).

It is interesting to note that *inwards* means the animal's internal organs, i.e. the viscera and the viscera does not normally include the brain seeing it is an organ remote from the rest of the innards. Consequently, the ram's brains were not placed upon the altar with the rest of the rams inwards. It was removed from the head and set aside for the hide tanning process.

For those who doubt, may I point out **"we** [those who have been redeemed] **have the mind of Christ." (1 Cor 2:16)** and Jesus came to do the will of God, not to do what he thought best:
"I [Jesus] come (in the volume of the book it is written of me,) to do thy will, O God." (Heb 10:7).
"By the which will we are sanctified through the offering of the body of Jesus Christ once *for all*."

(Heb 10:10).

Furthermore, we know that Jesus came to do His Father's will because He said:
**"I came down from heaven, not to do mine own will, but the will of him that sent me.
And this is the Father's will which hath sent me, that of all which he hath given me I should lose nothing, but should raise it up again at the last day.
And this is the will of him that sent me, that every one which seeth the Son, and believeth on him, may have everlasting life: and I will raise him up at the last day." (Jn 6: 38-40).**

Consequently, the ram's brains would not have been appropriate to have been included as part of the sacrifice.

In addition, the ram's bladder was emptied of its urine and the urine set aside as well. The urine was not included as part of the sacrifice because Jesus gives us living water.
"He that believeth on me, as the scripture hath said, out of his belly shall flow rivers of living water." (Jn 7:38).

Coats of Skins

Including the ram's urine as part of the sacrifice would have indicated that Jesus' blood needed cleansing of sin because the blood's impurities are removed by the kidneys with the resultant waste products stored in the bladder until the waste-water is passed.

Dung likewise, would not have been included as part of the sacrifice because there was no uncleanness found in Him and being the bread of Heaven there would be no impurities that needed to be eliminated.

In addition, the LORD used dung to illustrate His total contempt for those who forsake Him:
"If ye will not hear, and if ye will not lay *it* to heart, to give glory unto my name, saith the LORD of hosts, I will even send a curse upon you, and I will curse your blessings: yea, I have cursed them already, because ye do not lay *it* to heart.
Behold, I will corrupt your seed, and spread dung upon your faces, *even* the dung of your solemn feasts;" (Mal 2:2-3).

So, including it as part of the Burnt Offering would have been totally inappropriate because the Father clearly said;
"Thou art my beloved Son, in whom I am well

pleased." (Mat 1:11).

Step 10. Burnt to Ash

The ram's internal fat, (including the fat surrounding the kidneys), as well as the subcutaneous fat that was scraped from the hide was placed upon the wood that was on the altar.

The ram's internal fat represents physical health and vigor. Placing this internal fat on the altar served to illustrate that all should expend their energies in serving the Lord:

"The days of our years are, threescore years and ten; and if by reason of strength they be fourscore years, yet is their strength labour and sorrow; for it is soon cut off, and we fly away. ...
So teach *us* to number our days, that we may apply *our* hearts unto wisdom." (Psm 90:10-11).

It also served as an acknowledgment that it is the Lord that determines each person's health and vigor for **"Which of you by taking thought can add one cubit unto his stature?" (Mat 6:27).**

Placing the subcutaneous fat on the altar indicated that worldly possessions are not eternal. All possessions accumulated in this life, will at death, be left behind because, **"Naked came I out of my mother's womb, and naked shall I return thither: the LORD gave, and the LORD hath taken away; blessed be the name of the LORD." (Job 1:21).** More importantly, worldly possessions have absolutely no influence upon a soul's salvation.

Remember:
"the wicked shall perish, and the enemies of the LORD *shall be* **as the fat of lambs: they shall consume; into smoke shall they consume away" (Psm 37:20).**
"But as many as received him [Jesus Christ], to them gave he power to become the sons of God, *even* **to them that believe on his name:**
Which were born, not of blood, nor of the will of the flesh, nor of the will of man, but of God." (Jn 1:12-13).

After this, the dismembered, cleaned, and inspected components of the ram were placed in an orderly fashion upon the altar (excepting the hide, brains, urine, and dung) indicating that our Saviour would experience the full, unabated wrath of God in our stead. Then as Adam stood by **"there came a fire out from before the LORD, and consumed upon** the altar the burnt offering and the fat:" (Lev 9:24).

Adam, as all men would, stood in total astonishment as his blood sacrifice for sin was completely consumed by the LORD. Elijah too witnessed this same spectacular event:
"the fire of the LORD fell and consumed the burnt sacrifice, and the wood, and the stones, and the dust, and licked up the water that *was* **in the trench. And when all the people saw** *it*, **they fell on their faces: and they said, The LORD, he** *is* **the God; the LORD, he** *is* **the God" (1 Kings 18:38).**

This spectacle brought home the fact that **"the LORD thy God** *is* **a consuming fire,** *even* **a jealous God." (Deut 4:24)** and must have been so awe-inspiring that one can be sure that Adam knew beyond a shadow of a doubt that he would be **"reconciled to God by the death of his Son,"** and **"saved from wrath through him** [Jesus Christ]." **(Rom 5:9-10).**

The complete consummation of the sacrifice by the flames indicated that our sinless Redeemer would be found to be totally acceptable to God because He **"knew no sin" (2 Cor 5:21),** and He **"did no sin" (1**

Coats of Skins

Pet 2:22) and **"in him is no sin." (1 Jn 3:5).**

At the conclusion of the Burnt Offering Adam fully understood that Jesus Christ was **"slain from the foundation of the world." (Rev 13:8).**

Another thing Adam learned was:
"after he [Jesus Christ] had offered one sacrifice for sins for ever, sat down on the right hand of God;
From henceforth expecting till his enemies be made his footstool.
For by one offering he hath perfected for ever them that are sanctified." (Heb 10:12-14).

Furthermore, Adam now assuredly knew that it would only be **"through our Lord Jesus Christ, by whom we have now received the atonement." (Rom 5:11).**

Adam now most assuredly knew that Jesus Christ would pay his sin debt and be his Saviour.

The only thing that Adam did not know was when Jesus Christ would appear. Fortunately for us **"now once in the end of the world hath he [Jesus Christ] appeared to put away sin by the sacrifice of**

himself." (Heb 9:26) 2018 years ago.

Additionally, because Jesus Christ was sinless, his sacrifice was a sweet savor to the LORD. Jesus Christ endured the cross, despising the shame:
"And thou shalt burn the whole ram upon the altar: it *is* a burnt offering unto the LORD: it *is* a sweet savour, an offering made by fire unto the LORD." (Ex 29:18).

Step 11. Washing

With the God's complete acceptance of the sacrifice Adam knew for a certainty that ***"there is* one God, and one mediator between God and men, the man Christ Jesus; who gave himself a ransom for all, to be testified in due time." (1 Tim 2:5-6).** The LORD then proceeded to instruct Adam in the making of the coats of skins to further illuminate and drive home key aspects of salvation.

Making the coats of skins served to illustrate how regeneration saves a sinner's soul from eternal damnation in the Lake of Fire. These coats of skins were to be Adam and Eve's coats of righteousness and were to be made from the flayed, field-dressed, and salted hide of the Burnt Offering.

The first step was for Adam to take the salted hide and wash it in water to remove all the dirt and dust from the ram's coat, and any residual blood, fat and salt from the inner side. The necessity of washing was noted by Jesus when He said:
"If I wash thee not, thou hast no part with me." (Jn 13:8).

It was through this operation that the tough and rigid hide was re-hydrated and softened. It was washing whereby the hide became supple and workable and the picture of the **"washing of regeneration, and renewing of the Holy Ghost." (Titus 3:5)** can clearly been seen.

One can almost hear Adam cry:
**"Have mercy upon me, O God, according to thy loving kindness: according unto the multitude of thy tender mercies blot out my transgressions.
Wash me thoroughly from mine iniquity, and cleanse me from my sin. For I acknowledge my transgressions: and my sin *is* ever before me.
Against thee, thee only, have I sinned, and done *this* evil in thy sight:" (Psm 51:1-3).**

Once the Gospel of Christ, the good news has been

believed by faith, **"ye are washed, ... ye are sanctified, ... ye are justified in the name of the Lord Jesus, and by the Spirit of God." (1 Cor 6:11).** In short, your sins are completely washed away.

It is by this act of regeneration that we are cleansed of our sins. Therefore:
"Come now, and let us reason together, saith the LORD: though your sins be as scarlet, they shall be white as snow; thought they be red like crimson, they shall be as wool." (Isa 1:18).

Remember, it is **"Not by works of righteousness which we have done, but according to his mercy he [Jesus Christ] saved us, by the washing of regeneration, and renewing of the Holy Ghost;" (Titus 3:5).**

This washing of the word gives newness of life to a tired, troubled, and conflicted soul.
"Therefore if any man *be* in Christ, *he is* a new creature: old things are passed away; behold, all things are become new." (2 Cor 5:17).

Step 12. Fleshing

Coats of Skins

After a thorough washing Adam's next step was to flesh the hide. This process removes the fatty sub-tissue from the inner-side of the hide and the hair from the exterior thereby illustrating that Christians were to be considered the off scouring of the world.

"We *are* fools for Christ's sake, but ye *are* wise in Christ; we *are* weak, but ye *are* strong; ye *are* honourable, but we *are* despised.
Even unto this present hour we both hunger, and thirst, and are naked, and are buffeted, and have no certain dwelling place;
And labour, working with our own hands: being reviled, we bless; being persecuted, we suffer it:
Being defamed, we entreat: we are made as the filth of the world, *and are* the offscouring of all things unto this day." (1 Cor 4:10-13).

Fleshing was accomplished by draping the clean, wet hide over a smooth log inner-side up, about waist high. Then the excess flesh and fatty sub-tissue was systematically scraped off the inner surface using a large scraper.

Once that was accomplished, Adam turned the hide over and the ram's fur was wetted with the ram's urine that he had set aside. Urine loosens the fur making it easy to remove. When the hair fibers loosened, the hide was scraped to remove all the ram's hair and dermis.

Urine and dung are used in the Bible to show utter contempt:
"Behold I will corrupt your seed, and spread dung upon your faces, *even* **the dung of your solemn feasts; and** *one* **shall take you away with it.**
And you shall know that I have sent this commandment unto you, that my covenant might be with Levi, saith the LORD of hosts." (Mal 2:3-4).

An animal's fur is its glory and the use of urine to loosen the fur shows the LORD's utter contempt and disdain for mans self-glorification:
"No flesh should glory in his [God's] presence." (1 Cor 1:29)
because **"by the deeds of the law there shall no flesh be justified in his [God's] sight: for by the law** *is* **the knowledge of sin." (Rom 3:20).**

The Apostle Paul explains this lesson best in his *Epistle of Paul the Apostle to the Romans* Chapter 7, Verses 18:
"For I know that in me (that is, in my flesh,)

dwelleth no good thing:".

The removal of the fur and fatty sub-tissue served to illustrate the humbling effects of the Word of God. It also served show that **"Thy pomp is brought down to the grave," (Isa 14:11).**

Fleshing also presents a picture of the effect that preaching the Word of God has on the flesh. Preaching scrapes away our vainglory and prideful veneer thereby showing us how we stand in the eyes of Almighty God. *The Epistle of Paul the Apostle to the Philippians,* Chapter 3, Verse 3 reminds all that we are to **"have no confidence in the flesh."** and **"nothing *be done* through strife or vain glory;" (Phil 2:3).**

All should take heed to **"Talk no more so exceeding proudly; let *not* arrogancy come out of your mouth: for the LORD is a God of knowledge, and by him actions are weighed." (1 Sam 2:3).**

Remember:
"The fear of the LORD *is* to hate evil: pride, and arrogancy, and the evil way, and the forward mouth, do I [the LORD] hate." (Prov 8:13).

So, heed the warning, for the LORD has unequivocally stated:

"I will punish the world for *their* evil, and the wicked for their iniquity; and I will cause the arrogancy of the proud to cease, and will lay low the haughtiness of the terrible." (Isa 13:11).

He that hath ears to hear, let him hear.

Step 13. Bating

The scraped and hairless hide was then thoroughly kneaded in a mixture of dung and water and wrung out. This operation was known as bating. It was by this operation that God let it be known that while our souls may be saved by grace they still reside in sinful flesh.

One should never forget that even after the will of the flesh has been defeated and our souls have been regenerated, the will of the flesh remains a very formidable foe.

The Apostle Paul explains that the even though his soul was not subject to the will of the flesh, he was still unable to completely resist its influence because **"For I know that in me (that is, in my flesh,) dwelleth no good thing: for to will is present with**

me; but *how* to perform that which is good I find not.
For the good that I would I do not: but the evil which I would not, that I do.
Now if I do that I would not, it is no more I that do it, but sin that dwelleth in me." (Rom 7:18-20).

Hence rubbing the hide with the ram's dung until it was worked down into the hide, presented the perfect picture that from the LORD's viewpoint, our redeemed souls reside in fleshly bodies that are very nasty and very very sinful.

But not to worry, because the bating process was performed three times indicating that it is a God ordained promise that **"There hath no temptation taken you but such as is common to man: but God *is* faithful, who will not suffer you to be tempted above that ye are able; but will with the temptation also make a way to escape, that ye may be able to bear it."** (1 Cor 10:13).
Upon completion of the bating process, the hide was now properly prepared to readily absorb the tanning liquor.

Step 14. Tanning

After the bating process, Adam was instructed on how to tan the hide. Tanning requires that the bated hide be cured in tanning liquor and buffed. The tanning liquor was made by mashing the ram's brain that had been set aside during the dissection process into a pulp. The pulped brain was then mixed with water in a vat thereby producing a light gray slurry.

With the tanning liquor ready, Adam proceeded to tan the ram's hide:

> **First**, he soaked and kneaded the bated hide in the tanning liquor until the hide had completely absorbed the tanning liquor.
>
> **Secondly**, he lifted the saturated hide out of the vat, wrung out the excess liquor and then buffed it.

These two processing steps were performed 3 times in succession in order to completely tan the hide.

The tanning operation was performed three times thereby indicating that the LORD was the *prime* authority of salvation and it emphasized that the LORD desires all regenerated souls to **"have the mind of Christ." (1 Cor 2:16)** because the regenerated have received **"the spirit which is of**

God; that we might know the things that are freely given to us of God." and "he that is spiritual judgeth all things, yet he himself is judged of no man." (1 Cor 2:12 & 15).**

The fact that tanning is a two-step process also reminds us that Christians have to choose daily to crucify their flesh and give no quarter to the lusts of the flesh and the Devil.

Additionally, the brain and water slurry used in the tanning operation made it clear that **"Only the LORD give thee wisdom and understanding, ... that thou mayest keep the law of the LORD thy God." (1 Chron 22:12).**

God desires all **"that ye might be filled with the knowledge of his will in all wisdom and spiritual understanding;
That ye might walk worthy of the Lord unto all pleasing, being fruitful in every good work, and increasing knowledge of God;" (Col 1: 9-10).**

And this is accomplished **"Not by works of righteousness which we have done, but according to his mercy he saved us, by washing of regeneration, and renewing of the Holy Ghost;"**

(Titus 3:5).

Additionally, I am sure that those whose parents *tanned their hide* when they were young can surely attest, that they got their hide tanned because **"He that spareth his rod hateth his son: but he that loveth him chasteneth him betimes." (Prov 13:24)**

And likewise with the Lord:
"whom the Lord loveth he chasteneth, and scourgeth every son whom he receiveth.
If you endure chastening, God dealeth with you as with sons; for what son is he whom the father chasteneth not?
But if ye be without chastisement, whereof all are partakers, then are ye bastards, and not sons.
Furthermore we have had fathers of our flesh which corrected *us*, and we gave *them* reverence: shall we not much rather be in subjection unto the Father of spirits, and live?
For they verily for a few days chastened *us* after their own pleasure; but he for *our* profit, that *we* might be partakers of his holiness.
Now no chastening for the present seemeth to be joyous, but grievous: nevertheless afterward it yieldeth the peaceable fruit of righteousness unto them which are exercised thereby." (Heb 12:6-11).

Finally, it is interesting to note that frontiersmen have reported that all animals have just enough brains to tan their own hides. This fact provides an important corollary to all, in that the unregenerated man, left to his own devices has just enough brains to get his *hide tanned* by God Almighty at The Judgment. Consequently, all should earnestly seek salvation.

Step 15. Buffing

With the tanning liquor completely permeating the hide, it was wrung out and buffed. Buffing smooths and stretches the hide. The buffing operation required the damp hide be laid out on a flat horizontal surface. Then, with the use of a buffing stick, the hide was gently stretched and the naturally occurring lumps and bumps were massaged out.

The buffing stick was a long stick with a large bulbous end. The blunt, bulbous end helped ensured that the delicate hide would not be punctured or torn as the hide was stretched and massaged. After three buffings the hide was satin smooth and of uniform thickness.

Buffing was performed on the fragile and puncture

prone hide to illustrate that a **"bruised reed shall he not break, and smoking flax shall he not quench, till he send forth judgment unto victory." (Mat 12:20).**

Jesus Himself asks all to:
"Come unto me, all *ye* **that labour and are heavy laden, and I will give you rest.**
Take my yoke upon you, and learn of me; for I am meek and lowly in heart: and ye shall find rest unto your souls.
For my yoke *is* **easy, and my burden is light." (Mat 11:28-30).**

The tanning proceedings (soaking, kneading, wringing out, and buffing) were performed three times to ensure that the preserving (tanning) liquor permeated completely through the thickness of the hide.

Once again, this makes it very clear that the LORD is the *prime* causal agent of the changes seen in the life of all regenerated souls. Only the Gospel of Christ has the power to stretch our thoughts beyond the here and now. Only the Gospel of Christ provides us with the long view of life, and for a certainty, eternity is a long, long time.

Buffing, just like regeneration, knocks down our idiosyncrasies, quirks, and wierdnesses. It smooth's out mans personality thereby creating in us the ability to forgive and extend mercy to others.

Regeneration changes our walk. The Scriptures attest to its life changing effects:
"the fruit of the Spirit is love, joy, peace, longsuffering, gentleness, goodness, faith, Meekness, temperance: against such there is no law. And they that are Christ's have crucified the flesh with the affections and lusts." (Gal 5:22-24).

It is because **"the work of righteousness shall be peace; and the effect of righteousness quietness and assurance for ever." (Isa 32:17)** that we can be gracious and extend mercy to others, share the Gospel of Christ, and do good works.

Good works are important but be sure to note the distinction. No one can do *good works* unto salvation. Good works are a **result** of salvation because even **"the plowing [honest, hard work] of the wicked, *is* sin." (Prov 21:4)**.

In fact, until one's soul has been regenerated, nothing a person does can be considered *good work* because

"He that turneth away his ear from hearing the law, even his prayer *shall be* abomination." (Prov 28:9).

The effects that regeneration has on the soul are illustrated by the transformation that occurred to the demoniac of Gadarene. Jesus met the demoniac in his natural, unregenerated state:
"there met him out of the city a certain man, which had devils long time, and ware no clothes, neither abode in any house, but in the tombs." (Lk 8:27).

Jesus, **"according to his mercy saved him, by the washing of regeneration, and renewing of the Holy Ghost"** per *The Epistle of Paul the Apostle to Titus* Chapter 3, Verse 5, and the townsmen found him; **"sitting at the feet of Jesus, clothed, and in his right mind:" (Lk 8:35).**
When Jesus departed, He told the Gadarene:
**"Go home to thy friends, and tell them how great things the Lord hath done for thee, and hath had compassion on thee.
And he departed, and began to publish in Decapolis how great things Jesus had done for him: and all *men* did marvel." (Mk 5:19-20).**

Now, some people make the mistake of thinking that reformation is the same thing as regeneration. This is a very serious error because reformation can only make one a better person socially or outwardly. Reformation however cannot, does not, and never will be able to regenerate a person's soul and make them righteous.

Reformation, or *"getting religion"* as some call it, is incapable of achieve a definitive victory over the will of the flesh. This is why devout and highly religious people are never sure that they have *"done enough"* to merit entrance into Heaven and when asked: *"Are you going to go to Heaven when you die?"* The common reply is: *"I **hope** so"*.

All reformation can accomplish is the crafting of a new fig leaf apron as it were. This is why reformation is referred to as *"turning over a new leaf"*.

At the conclusion of the tanning process the hide is milk-white and forever soft, supple, and workable proving that the Gospel of Christ **"is the power of God unto salvation to every one that believeth;" (Rom 1:16).**

Via salvation, the LORD **"hath made us meet to be**

partakers of the inheritance of the saints in light:" and **"hath delivered us from the power of darkness, and hath translated *us* into the kingdom of his dear Son: In whom we have redemption through his blood, *even* the forgiveness of sins:" (Col 1:12-14)**.

However, one needs to be cognizant of the fact that if the hide is not properly tanned, it will dry out and once again become as stiff and inflexible as a sheet of plywood.

Adam's prayer that the LORD **"wash me, and I shall be whiter than snow." (Psm 51:7)** had been answered. Truly, the Lord, **"washed their robes, and made them white in the blood of the Lamb." (Rev 7:14)**.

Therefore, **"Come now, and let us reason together, saith the LORD: though your sins be as scarlet, they shall be white as snow; though they be red like crimson, they shall be as wool." (Isa 1:18)**.

Step 16. Sewing

With the tanned hides now white as newly fallen snow, satin smooth and fully pliable to the LORD's will Adam fashioned the hides into robes of righteousness for he and Eve.

For the sake of clarity, the above sacrifice and coat making process was enumerated as if Adam slew only one ram. However, it must certainly be true that Adam, in actuality, sacrificed multiple rams and tanned multiple hides in order to obtain enough tanned leather to make two coats of skins.

Under normal conditions, it takes four ram hides to make one coat. Consequently, Adam must have sacrificed at least eight rams. This is significant because 8 is the number for a new beginning, and certainly receiving a coat of righteousness from the LORD Himself provides man with a new beginning because **"if any man *be* in Christ, *he is* a new creature: old things are passed away; behold, all things are become new." (2 Cor 5:17).**

After all the hides were tanned, it is conjectured that God directed Adam and Eve to measure themselves. This is an important step because we must be honest in our assessment of how we measure up.
"LORD, make me to know mine end, and the measure of my days, what it is; that I may know how frail I am." (Psm 39:4).

110

Be sure to heed the warning:
"they measuring themselves by themselves, and comparing themselves among themselves, are not wise." (2 Cor 10:12).

Once their measurements were taken Adam cut the hides into the component pieces necessary to make two coats of skins. This served to illustrate the fact that **"the body [of regenerated believers] is one, and hath many members, and all the members of that one body, being many, are one body: so also is Christ.**
For by one Spirit are we all baptized into one body, whether *we be* Jews or Gentiles, whether *we be* bond or free; and have been all made to drink into one Spirit.
For the body is not one member, but many." (1 Cor 12:12-14).

After all the pieces were cut out, Adam then proceeded to stitch the many and varied pieces together. It should be noted that Christ is the head of the body of believers **"From whom the whole body fitly joined together and compacted by that which every joint supplieth, according to the effectual working in the measure of every part, maketh**

increase of the body unto the edifying of itself in love." (Eph 4:16).

When he was finished, he had one coat for himself and one coat for Eve. Each coat was custom tailored to achieve a proper fit illustrating that **"God set the members every one of them in the body, as it hath pleased him." (1 Cor 12:18)**
and **"That there should be no schism in the body; but *that* the members should have the same care one for another.**
And whether one member suffer, all the members suffer with it; or one member be honoured, all the members rejoice with it.
Now ye are the body of Christ, and members in particular." (1 Cor 12:25-27).

This tailoring mirrors each and every person's salvation experience. Each soul's salvation is unique in respect to time, place, and conditions surrounding the divine operation. And so, it is likewise for each person's robe of righteousness. Each is a perfectly tailored to cover a person's sins.

The key point to remember is that there is no such thing as a generic, common or universal salvation for mankind. No mortal can authorize the salvation of a person's soul. No mortal can save another person's soul. Salvation by anyone other than Jesus Christ is absolutely impossible.

Every person must repent of their sins and accept the free gift of salvation for themselves. Each soul is individually regenerated and each soul can only receive their own custom-made robe of righteousness from the eternal God-man, Christ Jesus. Salvation is an individual thing and you have only until you close your eyes in death to accept Jesus Christ as your personal Lord and Saviour.

Do not forget:
"if the wicked will turn from all his sins that he hath committed, and keep all my statutes, and do that which is lawful and right, he shall surely live, he shall not die.
All his transgressions that he hath committed, that shall not be mentioned unto him: in his righteousness that he hath done he shall live.
Have I any pleasure at all that the wicked should die? saith the Lord God: *and* **not that he should return from his ways, and live?**
… All his righteousness that he hath done shall not be mentioned: in his trespass that he hath trespassed, and in his sin that he hath sinned, in

them shall he die." (Ezek 18:21-24).

Step 17. Enrobing

Adam, like the prodigal son, surely admitted to his Father:
"Father, I have sinned against heaven, and in thy sight, and am no more worthy to be called thy son. But the father said to is servants, Bring forth the best robe and put it on him;" (Lk 15:21-22).

And so, with the tailor-made snow-white robes of righteousness now completed, the LORD graciously held them up as He assisted Adam and Eve with slipping them on illustrating that **"in him we live, and move, and have our being;" (Acts 17:28).**

It was by the mercy of God that Adam and Eve were not slain for their vain attempt to pay for their sins. It was only by the grace of God that they were now able to **"put on Christ" (Gal 3:27)** and **"your life is hid with Christ in God." (Col 3:3) "That in the ages to come he might shew the exceeding riches of his grace in *his* kindness toward us through Christ Jesus." (Eph 2:7).**

It was this final action whereby they both realized:

"there is neither bond or free, there is neither male nor female: for ye are all one in Christ Jesus.
And if ye *be* Christ's, then are ye Abraham's seed, and heirs according to the promise." (Gal 3:28-29).

Adam and Eve were once again restored to a state of righteousness. Their sinful souls were saved from eternal damnation in the Lake of Fire, and they knew **"the peace of God, which passeth all understanding, shall keep your hearts and minds through Jesus Christ." (Phil 4:7).**

One can be sure that both Adam and Eve declared: **"I will greatly rejoice in the LORD, my soul shall be joyful in my God; for he hath clothed me with the garments of salvation, he hath covered me with the robe of righteousness, as a bridegroom decketh himself with ornaments, and as a bride adorneth *herself* with her jewels." (Isa 61:10).**

From that day forward both said:
**"In God will I praise *his* word: in the LORD will I praise *his* word.
In God have I put my trust: I will not be afraid what man can do unto me.
Thy vows *are* upon me, O God: I will render**

praises unto thee.
**For thou hast delivered my soul from death:"
(Psm 56:10-13).**

Furthermore, every day thereafter, their coats of skins served as an ever-present reminder to;
"put ye on the Lord Jesus Christ, and make not provision for the flesh, to *fulfill* the lusts *thereof*." (Rom 13:14).

Making the coats of skins served to clothe Adam and Eve with robes of righteousness and the knowledge to instruct all future generations that **"he [God] hath made him [Christ Jesus] to be sin for us, who knew no sin; that we might be made the righteousness of God in him."** (2 Cor 5:21) because **"in Christ shall all be made alive." (1 Cor 15:22).**

Therefore, all should say:
"thanks *be* unto God, which always causeth us to triumph in Christ, and maketh manifest the savour of his knowledge by us in every place." (2 Cor 2:14).

Conclusion

Outfitted in tailor-made snow-white robes of

righteousness Adam and Eve's lesson in righteousness, grace, and mercy came to an end.

It was through this coat making process that the LORD had taught Adam and Eve:
"The law of the LORD *is* perfect, converting the soul: the testimony of the LORD *is* sure, making wise the simple.
The statutes of the LORD *are* right, rejoicing the heart: the commandment of the LORD *is* pure, enlightening the eyes.
The fear of the LORD *is* clean, enduring for ever: the judgments of the LORD *are* true *and* righteous altogether.
More to be desired *are they* than gold, yea, than much fine gold: sweeter also than honey and the honeycomb.
Moreover by them is thy servant warned: *and* in keeping of them *there is* great reward." (Psm 19:7-11).

Through the coat making process, Adam and Eve learned five valuable lessons that all men should take to heart:

1. **"He that trusteth in his own heart is a fool:" (Prov 28:26)** because **"There is a way which**

seemeth right unto a man, but the end thereof *are* the ways of death." (Prov 14:12)

2. "Woe unto *them that are* wise in their own eyes, and prudent in their own sight!" (Isa 5:21) because *"There is* no peace, saith the LORD, unto the wicked." (Isa. 48:22).

3. "the LORD *is* good; his mercy is everlasting; and his truth *endureth* to all generations." (Psm 100:5)

4. "Fear God, and keep His commandments: for this *is* the whole *duty* of man" (Ecc 12:13)

5. "the blood of Jesus Christ his Son cleanseth us from all sin." (1 Jn 1:7)

In closing, it is ordained that **"every one of us shall give account of himself to God."** (Rom 14:12).

Therefore, the question that all need to ask themselves is:

What will I be wearing when I close my eyes in death?

Will I be clothed in **"white raiment, that the shame of thy nakedness do not appear."**?

Or

Will I be **"clothed with shame"** in a self-made fig leaf apron?

And all the people said Amen, and Amen!

Postscript

Lay aside your garments that are stained with sin.

And be washed in the blood of the Lamb.

There is a fountain flowing for the soul unclean.

O, be washed in the blood of the Lamb.

Are you washed in the blood, in the soul cleansing blood of the Lamb?

Are your garments spotless?

Are they white as snow?

Are you washed in the blood of the Lamb?

If not, be sure you ask yourself this question before your eyes close in death:

"How shall [I] escape [Eternal Damnation in the Lake of Fire] if [I] neglect so great salvation; which at the first began to be spoken by the Lord, and was confirmed unto us by them that heard him; God also bearing them witness, both with signs and wonders, and with divers miracles, and gifts of the Holy Ghost, according to his own will?" (Heb 2:3-4).